The Joy of jQuery

A Beginner's Guide to the World's Most Popular JavaScript Library

by

Alan Forbes

The Joy of jQuery

Table of Contents

1

What is jQuery?

Introduction

jQuery is a programming language you can use to create cool web applications. It's free, powerful, relatively easy to set up and learn, and it has extensions and plugins available to do almost anything you could imagine. You can get started quickly, and you won't outgrow it later when you get really good at it. In my humble opinion, jQuery is well worth it the time and effort you put into learning it.

Frankly, it's just *plain fun* too. That's what inspired me to write this book.

Let's get started. The most basic concept you need to grasp is that a web page is just a bunch of text, organized in a certain way, which is displayed by a browser. The browser reads this text and builds a model of the page in memory called the 'document object model'. jQuery lets you manipulate the document object model (also commonly known as the 'DOM'). You will see the term DOM throughout this book.

jQuery is a lightweight JavaScript library with the tagline of "*write less, do more*". So what does that mean, exactly? To understand what it means, it helps to have an idea of what jQuery is intended to help you do. If you didn't have jQuery (or any other framework like Dojo, which is also **very** cool) then the way you would make things happen in the browser is to use a language called JavaScript.

JavaScript is programming language that is built into all modern web browsers so that client-side scripts can interact with the user, control the browser, communicate with the server in the background, and alter the document content and formatting that is displayed. JavaScript is a full-featured programming language and, as such, it can be rather complicated.

jQuery is written in JavaScript. In fact, jQuery is a *lot* of JavaScript all in one place-- hence the phrase 'library'. It's like a library **full** of JavaScript code. The purpose of jQuery is to make it easier for you to use JavaScript in your web pages. jQuery takes many of the common tasks that would otherwise require lots of lines of JavaScript code and turns them into methods that you can call with a single line of code. But of course, when your "one line" of code is executed, what *really* happens inside the browser is that all the code in the jQuery library is executed in its place. That's what jQuery saves you from --- writing all the JavaScript that is 'under the hood'.

> jQuery is a language that converts your **one line of simple code** into dozens and possibly even hundreds of lines of **complex** JavaScript code. It does this automatically and nearly instantaneously. In fact, that is the **whole point** of jQuery.

jQuery simplifies a lot of the complicated things from JavaScript, like AJAX calls and DOM manipulation. The jQuery library contains the following core features:

- HTML/DOM manipulation

- CSS manipulation

- HTML event methods

- Effects and animations

- AJAX

- Utilities

In addition, jQuery also has plugins that can likely solve any problem you are facing.

What jQuery is NOT

You have to use jQuery for what it is good for. As we have described it, jQuery is a language used for manipulating web pages *after* they have been sent to the browser. Because it only works with the HTML in the browser, we call this a **client** scripting tool. 'Client' is just a fancy word meaning 'browser' in this context but I mention it because it is an industry term.

jQuery is not a server scripting language. A server scripting language is one that runs on the web server, and manipulates the HTML before it is sent to the browser. A good example of a server scripting language is PHP. If you would like to learn about manipulating HTML before it even gets to the browser, please check out the companion book 'The Joy of PHP'.

A **client** scripting language (such as jQuery) manipulates HTML *after* it has been sent to the browser.

A **server** scripting language (such as PHP) manipulates HTML *before* it has been sent to the browser.

Adding jQuery to Your Web Pages

There are two ways to start using jQuery on your web site. You can:

1. Download the jQuery library from jQuery.com or,

2. Include jQuery from a CDN, such as Google

Downloading jQuery

There are two versions of jQuery available for downloading: the production version and the development version.   The production version is for your live website because it has been minified and compressed. The production version is fast, but virtually incomprehensible to humans. The development version is intended only for testing and development. The development version is uncompressed and consists of human-readable code.   But of course, it's slower to load. Both versions can be downloaded from jQuery.com.

The jQuery library is a single JavaScript file, and you reference it with the HTML <script> tag which, in general, should be placed inside the <head> section of your HTML file, such as:

```
<head>
<script src="jquery-1.10.2.min.js"></script>
</head>
```

Tip: Place the downloaded file in the same directory as the pages where you wish to use it.

Do you wonder why we do not have to specify the **type="text/javascript"** inside the <script> tag anymore? In fact, this is no longer required in HTML5. JavaScript is the default scripting language in HTML5 and in all modern browsers!

Alternatives to Downloading

Both Google and Microsoft host jQuery. To use jQuery from Google or Microsoft, use one of the following:

Google CDN:

```
<head>
<script src="http://ajax.googleapis.com/ajax/libs/jquery/1.10.2/jquery.min.js">
</script>
</head>
```

If you look at the Google URL above you'll see that the version of jQuery is specified in the URL (1.10.2). If you would like to simply use the latest version of jQuery, you can either remove a number from the end of the version string (for example 1.10), then Google will return the latest version available in the 1.10 series (1.10.0, 1.10.1, etc.), or you can take it up to the whole number (1), and Google will return the latest version available in the 1 series (from 1.1.0 to 1.10.2).

Microsoft CDN:

```
<head>
<script src="http://ajax.aspnetcdn.com/ajax/jQuery/jquery-1.10.2.min.js">
</script>
</head>
```

Using a hosted version of jQuery from Google or Microsoft offers some serious advantages to hosting it yourself. Many users will have already downloaded jQuery from Google or Microsoft when visiting a different site. As a result, they won't need to download it again because their browser will already have it stored locally. This leads to faster loading time of your site. Also, most CDN's will make sure that when a user requests a file it will be served from the server closest to them, which may well be closer (and more importantly faster) than your server.

> Unless you have a compelling reason to host jQuery yourself, you should use a CDN (Content Delivery Network).

Source Code

You can get all the source code that accompanies this book by visiting http://www.thejoyofjquery.com and joining the mailing list. I'll never spam you, and you can always opt out if you lose interest. Although I haven't done any yet, I do intent to make some youtube videos of the source code in action and I'll update everyone on the mailing list as they come out.

Contacting the Author

I invite you to contact me if you have any book feedback (such as typos or code bugs) or questions. If there's something you just don't get, maybe other people will have the same issue and it means I need to improve that particular section. I take the time to get back to everyone who emails me. I'm at AlanForbes@outlook.com

Installing for a Web Site

If you want to make your application you want to be available to everybody via the Internet, you'll need to install your application onto a publicly accessible server. Typically that means finding a hosting provider.

If you are looking for an inexpensive hosting provider, my own PHP-based site (which makes it easy for people to write their own Kindle books at http://www.KindleSmith.com) is hosted at AccuWeb Hosting, and I haven't had any problems with them.

If you'd like to use them too, I would appreciate if you use my affiliate link at https://manage.accuwebhosting.com/aff.php?aff=743

Using the above link won't cost you any more, and I'll get a small commission on the sale. Thank you.

2

Getting Started with jQuery

Basic jQuery Syntax

With jQuery you select (query) HTML elements and perform "actions" on them.

jQuery Syntax

The jQuery syntax is designed for selecting HTML elements and then performing some action on them.

The basic syntax is: $(selector).action()

- The $ sign means 'what follows is jQuery'

- The (selector) is used to find (or select) a subset of HTML elements

- The action defines what will happen to the selected elements.

Here's a picture that points out each element:

Inside the parenthesis is a selector that selects the desired page elements

$(selector).action()

$ sign means 'what follows is jQuery'

The action defines the operation to be performed

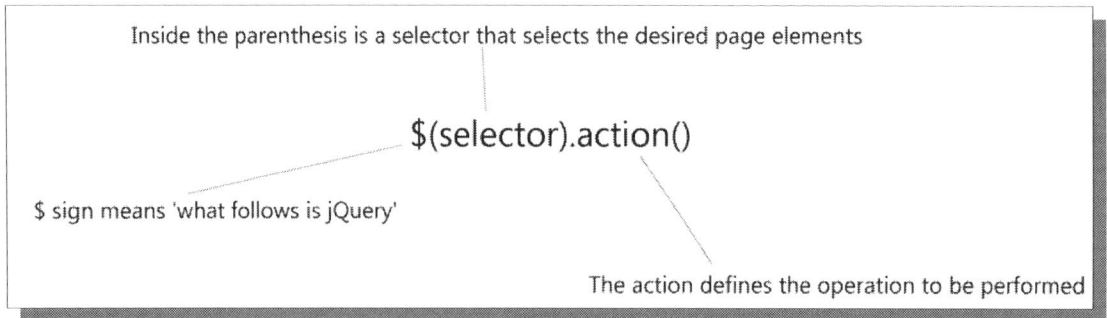

jQuery Examples

$(this).hide() - hides the current element.

$("p").hide() - hides all <p> elements.

$(".test").hide() - hides all elements with class="test".

$("#test").hide() - hides the element with id="test".

Are you familiar with CSS selectors? If so, you are in luck. jQuery uses CSS syntax to select elements. You will learn more about the selector syntax in the next chapter of this tutorial.

The Document Ready Event

You might have noticed that all jQuery methods in our examples, are inside a document ready event:

```
$(document).ready(function(){
   // jQuery methods go here...
});
```

This is to prevent any jQuery code from running before the document is finished loading (i.e., before it is ready).

It is good practice to wait for the document to be fully loaded and ready before working with it. This also allows you to have your JavaScript code before the body of your document, in the head section.

Here are some examples of actions that can fail if methods are run before the document is fully loaded:

Trying to hide an element that is not created yet

Trying to get the size of an image that is not loaded yet

Tip: The jQuery team has also created an even shorter method for the document ready event:

```
$(function(){
  // jQuery methods go here...
});
```

Use the syntax you prefer. We think that the document ready event is easier to understand when reading the code.

3

Introduction to HTML

Introduction

As we have described it, jQuery is a language used for manipulating web pages **after** they have been sent to the browser. Web pages are written in HTML, and jQuery is used so that the HTML on a given page can change dynamically depending on certain situations that you define.

Since jQuery is used to **manipulate** the HTML on a page, it only makes sense that you need to understand basic HTML before you can go any further.

Cascading Style Sheets (CSS) is a related technology used to define the look and feel of an HTML page. Sometimes CSS is referred more simply as a style sheet.

jQuery allows you to manipulate a web page's HTML and CSS. If you already understand HTML and CSS **very well**, you can skip the next two chapters. If you think you could benefit from a quick refresher on these baseline technologies then please take the time to read them now, because jQuery isn't going to make much sense otherwise.

Basic HTML

HTML is the primary building block of the web and so it is crucial to have a basic understanding of what HTML is and how it works. HTML is a markup language that is used by browsers so that they know how to render a document as a web page. Regardless of whether a document starts off as HTML written by hand or is generated using ASP, JSP, or PHP, *ultimately* the document is turned into HTML and sent to the browser to be rendered for display to a person.

HTML is a markup language that defines the structure and outline of a web page. Markup is not intended to define the look and feel of the content on the page beyond rudimentary concepts such as headers, paragraphs, and lists.

The presentation attributes of HTML have all been deprecated, which is a fancy way of saying 'please don't use these anymore, even though they still work'. The current best practices in HTML page design stipulate that most style should be contained in style sheets, which are a set of rules that describe how a page should look. Style sheets are a topic in themselves, and covered in the next chapter.

Writing and viewing HTML is incredibly easy (and fun), which of course is a big factor in what made it so popular. If you are reading this document on a computer, then you already have **everything** you need to try it out right now. All you need to build a web page (an HTML page) is a computer, a text editor (something as simple as Notepad will suffice) and a browser. To work with HTML you don't need a server or any special software at all. You simply create the file, save it with an .htm or .html extension, and open it directly in your browser.

> Windows users will find Programmer's Notepad to be a great editor for

creating HTML files.

Basic Elements of HTML

All HTML based documents have the same basic elements. They are composed of tags that define the various parts of the document—from where it starts and ends to everything in between. HTML uses elements ("tags") to mark up sections of text. These can include headings, subtitles, lists, bold or underlined text and, of course, links. HTML documents read from left to right and top to bottom.

Tags

To distinguish tags from ordinary text, tags appear inside brackets: < and >. Most tags have an open and close tag, also known as a start and end tag. The open tag starts with < and end tag starts with </. For example **** indicates to start bold and **** indicates to stop (end) bold.

For example here is a paragraph element:

```
<p>This is the first paragraph.</p>
```

In this example the **<p>** and **</p>** are the tags; they are used to delineate the text contained within as a paragraph. Something worth pointing out here is that you don't have to put everything on a single line. The code above works just as well as this below:

```
<p>
  This is the first paragraph
</p>
```

In fact, the indentation isn't needed either, although it certainly improves the readability. Keep in mind that someone (maybe you) may have to edit your

HTML in the future so making it readable is a good idea.

All tag formats are the same. They begin with a less-than sign: < and end with a greater-than sign: >. Always. What goes inside the < and > is the tag name. A big part of learning HTML is learning the specific tags and what they do.

Nested Tags

In general, most tags can be nested inside other tags, but of course there may be exceptions to this rule.

Here you see the bold tag nested inside of a paragraph tag:

```
<p>
  This is the first paragraph, with some <b>bold</b> text in it.
</p>
```

Not all elements have both an opening and closing piece. For example, <br> doesn't have a corresponding </br>, and neither does <hr>.

> The <hr> tag inserts a horizontal rule (line) and the <br> tag inserts a new line.

Required tags

An HTML page starts with the <html> tag and ends with </html>. The body of the page goes inside body tags.

```
<!DOCTYPE html>
<html>
<body>
<p>This is my first paragraph.</p>
</body>

</html>
```

DocType

If a webpage is missing a <DOCTYPE> tag or has some sort of "transitional" doctype tag, the page will be rendered in what is called 'quirks' mode. Quirks mode is somewhat unpredictable, and you don't always get what you expect.

So, it is important to have a doctype tag if you want your web page to display in Standards mode, as expected. For simplicity, however, the examples in the book will skip this.

Head

The head of the document is where the **Title** and **Meta** information will go. Generally, you would also put any CSS styles, script tags, and link tags to external files in the Head also, if you have any.

```
<!DOCTYPE html>
<html>
<head>
 <title>
  This is the title of the page.
 </title>
</head>
<body>
 The body text goes here.
</body>
</html>
```

Optional Tags

Meta Tags

The Meta tag, along with the link tag, are unique in that they are the only HTML tags that require neither a closing tag nor a closing / at the end of the tag and are still considered syntactically correct.

The other thing about meta tags is that they are the only tag that, generally speaking, has no effect on the layout or processing of the page; they are used to give information about the page and/or site being viewed. The meta tag is essentially a key/value pair, and each tag can only contain one pair of values. Meta tags are used primarily by search engines.

Useful Tags

Headers

Headers are used to organize information into hierarchical groupings.

<h1>Heading1</h1>

<h2>Heading2</h2>

<h3>Heading3</h3>

<h4>Heading4</h4>

<h5>Heading5</h5>

<h6>Heading6</h6>

Header tags are block-level elements, meaning they take up an entire line by themselves, and no other markup is allowed inside heading tags.

DIV

The DIV tag is one you can use to create a logical division within your document. DIVs work with CSS, and allow you to write CSS rules that specify how the text within the DIV should be formatted.

Images/Picture

To add an image to your document, you use the "image" tag. To insert an image into your html document use the following syntax:

```
<img src="smiley.gif" alt="Smiley face">
```

The value that you put in the 'src=' attribute can either specify a graphic that is on the local file system, or you can specify a full URL which retrieves the image from somewhere else on the Internet.

Links

A link takes a user to another place when they click on it. The link can be to a specific part of the open document or to a new page entirely.

Takes the user to a new page.

```
<a href="http://www.joyofphp.com">Visit Joy of PHP!</a>
```

Takes the user to a different place (as indicated by the tag <a id="top">) in the current page:

```
<a href="#top">Go to top</a>
```

Lists

There are two kinds of lists— ordered and unordered. An **ordered** list is numbered, such as 1, 2, 3, while an **unordered** list is a list of bullet items. There are tags to start and stop the list, and tags for each item in the list.

An ordered list starts with the <ol> tag. An unordered list starts with the <ul> tag. Each list item, regardless of list type, starts with the <li> tag and ends with </li>.

```
<ul>
<li>Coffee</li>
<li>Milk</li>
</ul>
```

An ordered list:	An unordered list:
1. The first list item	• Coffee
2. The second list item	• Tea
3. The third list item	• Chocolate Milk

Exercise

Make a couple of basic HTML files and place them in the correct location on your computer so that you can open them in a browser. Include lists, paragraphs, and both bold and italic text. I haven't told you how to make task italic. Given that the tag for bold is <b>, what do you suppose is the tag for italic?

HTML Tables

Tables are awesome. They solve a lot of problems, but should not be used for *overall* page layout. HTML tables should only be used for rendering data that belongs in a grid or in other words where the data describe a number of objects that have the same properties. For example, if it makes sense to display the data in Microsoft Excel, use a table.

Tables are defined with the <table> tag. A table is divided into rows (with the <tr> tag), and each row is divided into data cells (with the <td> tag). td stands for "table data," and holds the content of a data cell. A <td> tag can contain text, links, images, lists, forms, other tables, etc.

Table Example

```
<table border="1">
<tr>
<td>row 1, cell 1</td>
<td>row 1, cell 2</td>
</tr>
<tr>
<td>row 2, cell 1</td>
<td>row 2, cell 2</td>
</tr>
</table>
```

This is how the HTML code above will look once translated by a browser. The browser will draw lines around the cells because I included border='1' in the opening <table> tag.

row 1, cell 1	row 1, cell 2
row 2, cell 1	row 2, cell 2

HTML Tables and the Border Attribute

If you do not specify a border attribute, the table will be displayed without borders. Sometimes this can be useful, but most of the time, we want the borders to show.

To display a table without borders, just drop the border attribute:

```
<table>
<tr>
<td>Row 1, cell 1</td>
<td>Row 1, cell 2</td>
</tr>
</table>
```

HTML Table Headers

Headers in a table (the top row which *describes* the data rather than *being* the data) are defined with the <th> tag.

All major browsers display the text in the <th> element as bold and centered.

```
<table border="1">
<tr>
<th>Header 1</th>
<th>Header 2</th>
</tr>
<tr>
<td>row 1, cell 1</td>
<td>row 1, cell 2</td>
</tr>
<tr>
<td>row 2, cell 1</td>
<td>row 2, cell 2</td>
</tr>
</table>
```

How the HTML code above looks in your browser:

Header 1	Header 2
row 1, cell 1	row 1, cell 2
row 2, cell 1	row 2, cell 2

Tables can create accessibility problems. Because tables are inherently meant to be read left to right, one row at a time, using them for layout can cause screen readers to read content out of order and cause confusion for the users who rely on screen readers.

HTML Forms

HTML forms are a special kind of HTML page that can be used to pass data to a server. Once the server gets the data, it may manipulate the data and send some of it back, or it may store it into a database for later use.

An HTML form will contain input elements like labels, text fields, check boxes, radio-select buttons, submit buttons, and more. A form can also present lists, from which the user can make a selection, or a text area where multi-line typing is allowed.

The basic structure of a form is as follows:

```
<form>
.
input elements
.
</form>
```

The form tags go inside the <body> tag. The data in the form is sent to the page specified in the form's action attribute. The file defined in the action attribute usually does something with the received input:

```
<form name="input" action="PostSignup.php" method="get">
```

We'll cover the form actions later.

The Input tag

The most common form element is the <input> element, which is used to collect information from the user. An <input> element has several variations, which depend on the **type** attribute. An <input> element also has a name element, so you can refer to it later. In general, the syntax is:

```
<input type="type" name="name"/>
```

An <input> element can be of type text, checkbox, password, radio button, submit button, and more. The common input types are described.

Text Fields: <input type="text"> defines a one-line input field that a user can enter text into:

```
<form>
First name: <input type="text" name="firstname"/><br>
Last name: <input type="text" name="lastname"/>
</form>
```

This is how the above HTML code would look in a browser:

First name:
Last name:

Password Field: <input type="password"> defines a password field. The password field is just like the text field, except the text that is typed in is not displayed on the screen.

```
Password: <input type="password" name="pwd"/>
```

Note that a password field doesn't secure the data, it only hides it on the screen.

Radio Buttons: <input type="radio"> defines a radio button. Radio buttons let a user select one (and only one) of a limited number of presented choices:

```
<body>
<form>
Pick your favorite color: <br/>
<input type="radio" name="color" value="red"/>Red<br/>
<input type="radio" name="color" value="blue"/>Blue<br/>
<input type="radio" name="color" value="green"/>Green
</form>
</body>
```

This is how the HTML code above looks in a browser:

Pick your favorite color:
- ⊙ Red
- ⊙ Blue
- ⊙ Green

Checkboxes: <input type="checkbox"> defines a checkbox. Checkboxes let a user select ZERO or MORE options of a limited number of choices.

```
<form>
<input type="checkbox" name="vehicle" value="Bike">I have a bike<br>
<input type="checkbox" name="vehicle" value="Car">I have a car
</form>
```

Submit Button: <input type="submit"> defines a submit button.

A submit button is used when the user has filled in the form, and is ready to send ("submit") the data they have entered to the server. The data is sent to the page specified in the form's action attribute, which will be covered in the next section.

HTML Form Actions & Methods

When you define a form, there are two required attributes: action and method. The action attribute (**action=**) indicates the name of the file that the form will be submitted to. The method attribute (**method=**) specifies *how* the form will be submitted.

The file defined in the action attribute usually does something with the received input, like put it into a database or send back some of the values to the user. Here's an example of a simple form with action and method attributes.

```
<form name="input" action="form_action.php" method="get">
Your name: <input type="text" name="name"/>
<input type="submit" value="Submit">
</form>
```

For the purposes of this book we will assume that the action attribute specifies the name of a PHP file. As you will see, the PHP file specified in the action attribute will have access to all the values in the form that was submitted.

4

Introduction to CSS

What is CSS?

CSS is an acronym that stands for <u>C</u>ascading <u>S</u>tyle <u>S</u>heets. *Styles* define how to display HTML elements, and a *Style Sheet* is a list of styles. For instance, you may have a style that defines how <h1> elements should look and another for how basic paragraphs should look.

> All browsers support CSS today. Learn it, love it.

Best practices dictate that a style sheet should be stored as a separate file that is distinct from the HTML page, although this is not the only supported configuration. Your style sheet should have a .css extension to make it easy to identify by both computers and humans.

Styles were added to HTML 4.0 to solve a problem. The problem was that HTML was *never intended* to contain tags for **formatting** a document. HTML was intended to define the **content** of a document, such as:

```
<h1>This is a heading</h1>
<p>This is a paragraph.</p>
```

When tags like <font>, and color attributes were added to the HTML 3.2 specification, it inadvertently created a real mess for web developers. While it was great to have such control over how a web page looked, the development of large web sites suddenly got a lot more tedious and expensive. To get that unique 'corporate identity' that marketers craved, fonts and color information were now required to be added to **every** page. Even worse, changing something that should be simple (i.e., all headers should now be in orange – as is the case on Amazon.com) meant editing every page. Again. Ugh.

To solve this problem, the World Wide Web Consortium (W3C) created CSS. In HTML 4.0, all formatting could be removed from the HTML document and stored in a separate CSS file.

> External Style Sheets can save a lot of work
>
> External Style Sheets are stored in CSS files

A Simple Style Sheet

An external style sheet is ideal when the style is applied to many pages, and this is the only type of style sheet we will cover in this book. With an external style sheet, you can change the look of an **entire web site** just by changing the contents of this one file.

An external style sheet can be written in any text editor because it is just a plain text file. Here's an example of a very basic style sheet:

```
body
{
background-color:#F7F8E0;
}
```

```
h1
{
color:orange;
text-align:center;
}
p
{
font-family:"Times New Roman";
font-size:20px;
}
```

CSS Style Rule Syntax

A style sheet consists of a number of Style Rules. These rules follow a simple format:

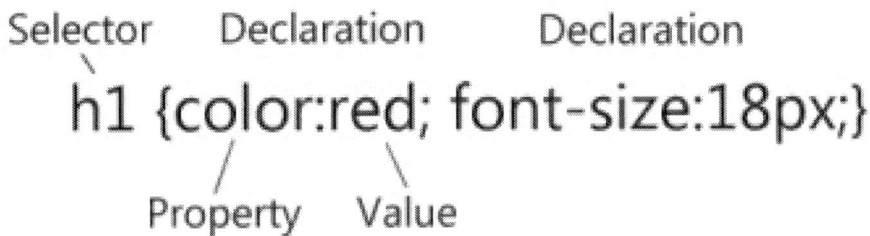

Selector   Declaration   Declaration

h1 {color:red; font-size:18px;}

Property   Value

A CSS rule has two main parts: a selector, and one or more declarations contained inside curly brackets. Let's use an example:

```
p
{
font-family:"Times New Roman";
font-size:12px;
}
```

The selector is normally the HTML element you want to style. In this case, we are selecting the paragraph elements "p".

Declarations occur after the selector and appear {between curly brackets}. Each declaration consists of a property and a value. The property is the style attribute you want to change, while the value is what you want to change it to.

 If you have multiple declarations, you separate them with a semi colon. In our example above, we set two attributes: font-family and font-size.

According to this rule, all the paragraphs will be Times New Roman, 12 points.

How to *use* a Style Sheet

OK, so now we have a style sheet. How do we use it? To use a style sheet, the HTML page simply has to link to the style sheet using the <link> tag. The <link> tag goes inside the head section, as shown:

```
<head>
     <link rel="stylesheet" type="text/css" href="mystyle.css">
</head>
```

If you used the above style sheet, the following changes to the document would occur:

1. The background color would change to light yellow (F7F8E0).
2. The h1 header would be orange and centered.
3. All the text within paragraphs would be 20 points and in the Times Roman font

Take a look back at the style sheet. Can you figure out *why* these changes would occur?

Selectors

As you might guess, selectors are not just limited to selecting single items, such as the paragraph tag. There are many CSS selectors. Here are a few:

CSS Selector Syntax	Description
*	Selects all the elements.
Tag Name	Selects all the elements with the HTML tag name 'TagName'. For example, valid tag names include p, h1, div, h2, li, etc.
.ClassName	Selects all the elements with the class name of 'ClassName'
#idName	Selects all the element with the ID name idName. Remember, ID names are supposed to be unique.
TagA TagB	Selects all the elements with tag name 'TagB' that are descendants of 'TagA'. For example , DIV P would select all the paragraphs inside a DIV tag.
TagA>TagB	Selects all the elements with tag name 'TagB' that are **direct** children of 'TagA'.

We'll cover more of these selectors when we talk about jQuery selectors, which are based on CSS selectors.

Child vs Descendant

You may notice that some selectors refer to an elements' descendant or children. Consider the following ancestor selector:

div p

This selects all paragraphs that are descendants of a div. (In other words, if a paragraph is inside a div, even it is first nested inside something else.

Then the child selector:

div > p

What's the difference? The difference is that the child selector only selects the immediate children, not the children of children.

CSS Declarations

The *second* half of a style is the declaration.   The declaration is the part that changes the selected item-- for instance, changing the color. Each declaration consists of a property and a value. The property is the style attribute you want to change, and the value is what you want to set it to.   In other words, if you were changing some text to blue, the property would be 'color' and the value would be 'blue'.

CSS Examples

Here's a basic example that sets the color of the text in paragraphs to blue:

```
p {color:blue;}
```

A CSS declaration always ends with a semicolon, and the declaration, or declaration groups are surrounded by curly brackets {}. If we wanted to make more than one change to the paragraph text, we would use a declaration group, such as:

```
p {color:blue;text-align:left;}
```

here's a more advanced example:

```
h1 { display: block; margin: 20px 0 6px 0;  font-size: 1.8em;  color: blue; text-decoration: none; text-align: center; }
```

You may have noticed that the second example was considerably harder to read because it reads like a run-on sentence. To make the CSS more readable to humans, it much better if you put each declaration on its own line, like this:

```
p
{
color:red;
text-align:center;
}
```

I highly recommend that you get into the habit of putting declarations on their own line, and err on the side of readability. You'll be glad you did.

CSS Comments

Speaking of readability, all proper programming languages support comments and CSS is no exception. Comments are used to explain your code, and are sure to help you when you edit the source code at a later date and can't remember why you did something a certain way or what the intent of a particular rule was. (How's that for a run-on?) Comments are ignored by browsers, but praised by users. Get in the comment habit too. :)

A CSS comment begins with "/*", and ends with "*/", like this:

```
/*Here I set the default formatting for paragraphs*/
p
{
text-align:center;
color:black;
font-family:Arial;
}
```

See how much easier to read that is?

Specifying Fonts

You may have noticed that many declarations mention fonts. The right font makes a significant difference in how a page looks. The font-family property can hold several font names at once and doing so is a best practice to ensure maximum compatibility. If the browser does not support the first font, it tries the next font, and so on.

Start with the specific font you really want, and end with a generic font family you can live with. This approach will instruct the browser to pick a font in the generic family if the preferred fonts are not available.

Example:

p{font-family:"Times New Roman", Times, serif}

Using CSS to Position Elements

Introduction to Positioning

The CSS positioning properties allow you to precisely position an element on a page. It can place an element on top of another, beside another, and even specify what should happen if an element's content is too big.

Elements can be positioned using the top, bottom, left, and right properties. However, these properties will not work unless the position property is set first. These properties also work differently depending on the positioning method.

There are four different positioning methods: Static, Fixed, Relative, and Absolute.

Static Positioning

HTML elements are positioned statically by default. A **static** positioned element is positioned on the page according to the "normal flow" of the page. In other words, when an element is static, it just goes with the flow. If you don't specify an element's position, then it is static.

Static positioned elements are not affected by the top, bottom, left, and right properties.

Fixed Positioning

An element with a **fixed** position is positioned relative to the browser window. It will not move when the page is scrolled because it is not positioned relative to any other elements on the page.

Here's an example of fixed positioning:

```
p.fixed
{
position:fixed;
top:25px;
right:15px;
}
```

This style will select paragraphs with the class 'fixed'. Fixed positioned elements are removed from the normal flow of things. All the other elements on the page behave as if fixed position elements simply do not exist.

Relative Positioning

A relative positioned element is positioned relative to where it **would otherwise be** if it were static. For instance, we could move an h2 element left or right of its usual position by modifying its left position.

For relatively positioned elements, the **left** property sets the left edge of an element to the left/right to its normal position.

The following rule moves the h2 elements left or right, depending on which class they belong to. For instance <h2 class='move_left'>

```
h2.move_left
{
position:relative;
left:-30px;
}
h2.move_right
{
position:relative;
left:30px;
}
```

The content of relatively positioned elements can be moved and can overlap other elements, but the space for the element is still preserved in the normal flow.

```
h2.pos_top
{
position:relative;
top:-50px;
}
```

Relatively positioned elements are often used as container blocks for absolutely positioned elements.

Absolute Positioning

An absolute position element is positioned relative to the first parent element that has a position other than static. If no such element is found, the containing block is <html>.

```
h2
{
position:absolute;
left:100px;
top:150px;
}
```

Absolutely positioned elements are removed from the normal flow. The document and other elements behave as if absolutely positioned elements do not exist.

Absolutely positioned elements can overlap other elements. Let's discuss this next.

Overlapping Elements

When elements are positioned outside the normal flow, they can overlap other elements. When two elements overlap, how do you decide which element goes in front and which one goes in back? This is determined by a property called the z-index. (I imagine that someone named Zachary came up with the term.)

The z-index property specifies the "stack order" of an element. Think of a group of 3 blocks stacked on top of each other. The block at the top has the z-index of 3, and the block at the bottom would have the z-index of 1. Looking at the stack from above, the block on the top is the most visible, so you can think of that one as being at the front. The block on the bottom can be thought of as being at the back of the stack.

An element can have a positive or negative stack order:

```
img
{
position:absolute;
left:0px;
```

```
top:0px;
z-index:-1;
}
```

An element with higher z-index is placed in front of an element with a lower z-index.

Note: If two positioned elements overlap, without a z-index specified, the element positioned last in the HTML code will be shown on top.

5

jQuery Selectors

What are jQuery selectors?

The concept of jQuery **selectors** is one of the most important ones that you will need to master on your journey of understanding the world of jQuery. Selectors use CSS syntax to select a specific page element or set of elements that you can then perform an operation against.

Understanding jQuery selectors is the key to using the jQuery library most effectively. The good news is that if you have worked with CSS before, you already know most of what follows.

A jQuery statement typically follows the syntax pattern:

```
$(selector).methodName();
```

The selector is a string expression that identifies the set of page elements that will be operated upon by the jQuery methods that follow the dot. This chapter will focus on the selector, while later chapters will focus on the methods available.

Many of the jQuery operations can also be strung together:

```
$(selector).method1().method2().method3();
```

As an example, let's say that we want to hide the DOM element with the id value of goAway and to add class name incognito:

```
$("#goAway").hide().addClass("incognito");
```

Applying the methods is easy. Coming up with the correct selector expressions is where the science turns into an art form.

> A great online reference to jQuery selectors and actions can be found at http://oscarotero.com/jquery/

What Does a jQuery Selector Return?

When a jQuery selector is applied to a web page, what is *really happening* under the hood is that a complex JavaScript function is examining **every element** in the DOM.   As each element is examined it is compared against the selector.   Those DOM elements that match the selector are put aside into a 'special list' containing only the matches. Once the entire document has been examined, the list of matching elements is "returned" so that it can be manipulated.

As you are learning about jQuery-- and there are literally hundreds of resources where you may do this-- you may see this list of selected items referred to as the '*matched set*', the '*wrapped set*', or the '*result set*'.   They all mean the same thing-- that 'special list' that was put aside as the elements in the DOM were compared against the selector.

Personally, I prefer the term 'result set' because it is consistent with the idea that the selector is basically running a query against the document and sending back a result.   But just because I like the term result set doesn't mean I should set you up for confusion later. Understand that the terms are interchangeable and mean exactly the same thing. I may mix it up here and there as we go along, just to help keep you awake.

Types of jQuery selectors

There are three categories of jQuery selectors: **Basic CSS** selectors, **Positional** selectors, and **Custom jQuery** selectors.

The Basic Selectors are known as "find selectors" as they are used to find elements within the DOM. The Positional and Custom Selectors are "filter selectors" as they filter (or fine-tune) a set of elements.

Basic CSS Selectors

The following jQuery selectors follow standard CSS3 syntax for selectors. Any variation of the selectors below could be used as the selector parameter for the jQuery command of

$(**selector**).methodName();

jQuery Selector Syntax	Description
*	Selects all the elements.
Tag Name	Selects all the elements with the HTML tag name 'TagName'. For example, valid tag names include p, h1, div, h2, li, etc.
.ClassName	Selects all the elements with the class name of 'ClassName'

jQuery Selector Syntax	Description
#idName	Selects all the element with the ID name idName. Remember, ID names are supposed to be unique.
TagA TagB	Selects all the elements with tag name 'TagB' that are descendants of 'TagA'. For example , DIV P would select all the paragraphs inside a DIV tag.
TagA>TagB	Selects all the elements with tag name 'TagB' that are **direct** children of 'TagA'.
TagA+TagB	Selects all the elements with tag name 'TagB' that are **immediately preceded** by a sibling of tag name 'TagA'.
TagA~TagB	Selects all the elements with tag name 'TagB' that are **preceded** by any sibling of tag name 'TagA'.
TagA:has(TagB)	Selects all the 'TagA' elements that have at least one descendant with tag name 'TagB'.
TagA.ClassName	Selects all the 'TagA' elements with a class name of ClassName.
TagA[attribute]	Matches all elements 'TagA' that posses an attribute a of **any** value.

jQuery Selector Syntax	Description
TagA[attribute=value]	Matches all elements 'TagA' with an attribute a whose value is **exactly** value.
TagA[attribute^=value]	Matches all elements 'TagA' with an attribute a whose value **starts with** value.
TagA[attribute$=value]	Matches all elements 'TagA' with an attribute a whose value **ends with** value.
TagA[attribute*=value]	Matches all elements 'TagA' with an attribute a whose value **contains** value.

Real-life Examples of Selectors

$("p") selects all the <p> elements

$("h1") selects all the <h1> elements

$("div a") selects all the anchor tag (<a>) elements within <div> elements

$("p>div") selects all <div> elements that are direct children of <p> elements

$("div~h2") selects all <div> elements that are preceded by a <h2> element

$("p:has(b)") selects all the paragraph elements that contain some bold text.

$("div.className") selects all <div> elements with a class name of className.

$(".className ") selects all the elements with class name of className.

$("#IDvalue") selects the element with the id value of IDvalue.

$("img[alt]") selects all the images (<img> elements) that have an alt attribute.

$("a[href$=.pdf]") selects all the anchors that link to a PDF file. It selects all the <a> elements with an href attribute that ends with .pdf.

You can practice with jQuery selectors by visiting http://www.w3schools.com/jquery/trysel.asp?filename=trysel_basic&jqsel=p.intro,%23choose

Multiple Selectors

Multiple selectors can be combined into a single statement if you separate them with commas. For example, the selector $("ul, ol") will select all the list (<ul> and <ol>) elements.

> You can use multiple selectors in a single statement by separating them with commas.

Positional Selectors

Positional selectors select elements based upon the positional relationships between the elements. These selectors can be appended to any base selector (which we'll denote as 'BaseSelector') to filter the matches based upon position. If the base selector is omitted, it is assumed to be * (in other words, all the elements).

Syntax

jQuery Selector Syntax	Description
BaseSelector:first	Selects the first element on the page matching the base selector.
BaseSelector:last	Selects the last element on the page matching the base selector.
BaseSelector:first-child	Selects all elements matching the base selector that are first children.
BaseSelector:last-child	Selects all elements matching the base selector that are last children.
BaseSelector:only-child	Selects all elements matching the base selector that are only children.
BaseSelector:nth-child(n)	Selects all elements matching the base selector that are n-th ordinal children. Counting starts at 1.
BaseSelector:nth-child(odd|even)	Selects all elements matching the base selector that are even or odd ordinal children. The first child is considered odd (counting starts at 1).
BaseSelector:even	Selects the even elements matching the base selector.
BaseSelector:odd	Selects the odd elements matching the base selector.
BaseSelector:eq(n)	Selects the n-th element within the set of elements matching the base selector. Counting starts at 0.

jQuery Selector Syntax	Description
BaseSelector:gt(n)	Selects elements matching the base selector that that are greater than the n-th element (exclusive). Counting starts at 0.
BaseSelector:lt(n)	Selects elements matching the base selector that that are less than the n-th element (exclusive). Counting starts at 0.

Real-life Examples

$("p:first") selects the first paragraph on the page.

$("img[src$=.png]:first") selects the first <img> element on the page that has a src attribute ending in .png

$("button.small:last") selects the last <button> element on the page that has a class name of small

$("li:first-child") selects all <li> elements that are first children within their lists

$("a:only-child") selects all <a> elements that are the only element within their parent

$("li:nth-child(2)") selects all <li> elements that are the second item within their lists

$("tr:nth-child(odd)") selects all odd <tr> elements within a table

$("div:nth-child(5n)") selects every 5th <div> element

$("div:nth-child(5n+1)") selects the element after every 5th <div> element

$(".someClass:eq(1)") selects the second element with a class name of someClass

$(".someClass:gt(1)") selects all but the first two elements with a class name of someClass

$(".someClass:lt(4)") selects the first four elements with a class name of someClass

Note that the :nth-child selectors begin counting at 1, while most jQuery selectors, such as :eq, :gt and :lt begin with 0.

jQuery Custom Selectors

These selectors are provided by jQuery to allow for commonly used, or just plain handy, selections that were not anticipated by the CSS Specification. Like the Positional Selectors, these selectors filter a base matching set (which we denote with B). Omitting B is interpreted as the set of all elements. These selectors may be combined; see the examples for some powerful selector combinations.

jQuery Selector Syntax	Description
BaseSelector:enabled	Selects elements matching the base selector that are in the enabled state.
BaseSelector:button	Selects elements matching the base selector that are of any button type.
BaseSelector:input	Selects elements matching the base selector that are input controls-- such as \<input>, \<select>, \<textarea> and \<button> elements.

jQuery Selector Syntax	Description
BaseSelector:checkbox	Selects elements matching the base selector that are the input type checkbox. For example this selector would select <input type="checkbox" name="colors">
BaseSelector:image	Selects elements matching the base selector that are of the input type image.
BaseSelector:file	Selects elements matching the base selector that are of the input type file.
BaseSelector:radio	Selects elements matching the base selector that are of type input[type=radio].
BaseSelector:text	Selects elements matching the base selector that are of the input type text.
BaseSelector:password	Selects elements matching the base selector that are of the input type password.
BaseSelector:submit	Selects elements matching the base selector that are either of type input type=submit or button type=submit.
BaseSelector:reset	Selects elements matching the base selector that are of type input[type=reset] or button[type=reset].

jQuery Selector Syntax	Description
BaseSelector:hidden	Selects elements matching the base selector that are hidden.
BaseSelector:header	Selects elements matching the base selector that are headers <h1> through <h6>.
BaseSelector:not(f)	Selects elements matching the base selector that do not match the filter selector specified by not(). A filter selector is any selector beginning with a colon(:)
BaseSelector:parent	Selects elements matching the base selector that are parents of non-empty children.
BaseSelector:selected	Selects elements matching the base selector that are in the selected state. Only <option> elements may posses this state.
BaseSelector:animated	Selects elements matching the base selector that are currently under animated control via one of the jQuery animation methods.
BaseSelector:visible	Selects elements matching the base selector that are not hidden.

Examples

As you can see, jQuery selectors give you both power and flexibility to create a set of DOM elements (referred to as the *result set* or *matched set*) that you wish to operate upon with jQuery methods. Let's look at one more set of examples.

$("img:animated") selects all the image elements that are undergoing animation.

$(":button:disabled") selects all the buttons that are disabled.   This would be a handy way to enable them.

$("input:radio:checked") selects all radio elements that **are** checked.

$("option:not(:selected)") selects all unselected <option> elements.

$(":text:visible") selects all text fields that are visible.

$("#myForm button:not(.someClass)") selects all buttons from the <form> with the id of myForm that do not possess the class name someClass.

$("select[name=choices] :selected") selects the selected <option> elements within the <select> element named choices.

("p:contains(hello world)") selects all <p> elements that contain the text 'hello world'.

JavaScript Objects

JavaScript programmers in the audience will appreciate that the result set created by the application of a selector can be treated as a JavaScript array. Technically it *is* a JavaScript array that jQuery is shielding us from. Sometimes though it can be useful to use array indexing to directly access elements within the result set.

For example:

```
var element = $("img")[0];
```

will set the variable element to the first element in the matched set

Taking Action on a Result Set

While the jQuery selectors give us great flexibility in identifying which DOM elements are to be added to a result set, sometimes there are criteria that cannot be expressed by selectors alone. Also, in the course of jQuery method chaining we may wish to adjust the contents of the result set between method calls.   For these situations jQuery provides methods that operate not upon the *elements* within the result set, but on the *result set itself*. This section will discuss those methods.

Adding Elements to a Result Set

You can add additional elements to a result set using the .add() method.

add(*expression*)

The *expression* is a selector that specifies which elements are to be matched. Elements that match the selector will be added to the existing matched items.

Given a jQuery object that represents a set of DOM elements, the .add() method constructs a new jQuery object from the union of those elements in the result set and the ones passed into the method. The argument to .add() can be pretty much anything that $() accepts, including a jQuery selector expression, references to DOM elements, or an HTML snippet.

Removing Elements from a Result Set

What if we want to remove elements from the result set? That is the job of the not() method.

not(*expression*)

The *expression* is a selector that specifies which elements are to be matched. Elements that do **not** match the selector will be included in the result.

Given a jQuery object that represents a set of DOM elements, the .not() method constructs a new jQuery object from a subset of the matching elements. The supplied selector is tested against each element; the elements that do **not** match the selector will be included in the result.

Examples

```
$("body *").css("font-weight","bold")
.not("p").css("color","blue");
```

Makes all body elements bold, then makes all but the paragraph elements blue.

```
$("body *").css("font-weight","bold")
.not(anElement).css("color","blue");
```

Similar to the previous example except the element referenced by variable *anElement* is not included in the second set (and therefore not colored blue).

Finding Descendants

Sometimes it is useful to limit the search for elements to descendants of the previously identified elements in the result set. The find() method does just that:

find(*expression*)

> The *expression* is a selector that specifies which descendant elements are to be matched.

Unlike the previously examined methods, find() only accepts a selector expression as its argument. The elements within the existing matched set will be searched for descendants that match the expression. Any elements in the original matched set that match the selector are not included in the new set.

Given a jQuery object that represents a set of DOM elements, the .find() method allows us to search through the descendants of these elements in the DOM tree and construct a new jQuery object from the matching elements. The .find() and .children() methods are similar, except that the latter only travels a single level down the DOM tree.

The first signature for the .find() method accepts a **selector** expression of the same type that we can pass to the $() function. The elements will be filtered by testing whether they match this selector.

Example

```
$("div").css("background-color","blue")
.find("img").css("border","1px solid aqua");;
```

Selects all <div> elements, makes their background blue, selects all <img> elements that are descendants of those <div> elements (but not <img> elements that are not descendants) and gives them an aqua border.

Filtering Matched Sets

When really fine-grained control is required for filtering the elements of a matched set, the filter() method comes in handy:

> filter(selector)

The selector is an expression that specifies which elements are to be retained.

The filter function can also be passed a function, but that is beyond the scope of this book. When passed a selector, it acts like the opposite of not(), keeping those elements which match the selector (as opposed to excluding them).

```
$(".invisible").show()
.filter("img[src$=.gif]").attr("title","Hello world!");
```

The first line selects all elements with class name invisible and sets them to visible. The second line filters the set down to just GIF images, and assigns a title attribute to them.

6

Using jQuery for Form Validation

Introduction - Basic Form Validation

One of the primary uses of JavaScript is form validation. The idea is to prevent users from submitting forms that contain "invalid" data, however you define it. For instance, if a form asks a user for their email, wouldn't it be great to check to see if a valid email address was entered? JavaScript makes this possible, but jQuery makes it easy with the validation plugin, which can be found at http://plugins.jquery.com/validation/

Let's imagine the following simple input form that could be used to allow visitors to your website to provide some feedback about it. We'll start with a basic web form that does not have any validation.

A Form Without Validation

The code to produce this form is shown below and provided in the sample code as '**novalidation.html**'

Code

```
01  <!DOCTYPE html>
02  <html>
```

```
03  <head>
04    <style type="text/css">
05    * { font-family: Arial; }
06    label { width: 10em; float: left; }
07    input, textarea { width: 15em; }
08    .submit { margin-left: 13em; margin-top: 2em;}
09    </style>
10
11  </head>
12  <body>
13  <form id="comments" method="get" action="">
14    <fieldset>
15    <legend>A simple form with no validation or messages</legend>
16    <div>
17      <label for="name">Name</label>
18      <input id="name" name="name" />
19    </div>
20    <div>
21      <label for="email" style="height: 1px">E-Mail</label>
22      <input id="email" name="email" />
23    </div>
24    <div>
25      <label for="url">URL (optional)</label>
26      <input id="url" name="url" class="url" value="" />
27    </div>
28    <div>
29      <label for="ccomment">Your comment</label>
30      <textarea id="ccomment" name="comment"></textarea>
31    </div>
32    <div>
33      <input class="submit" type="submit" value="Submit"/>
34    </div>
35    </fieldset>
36  </form>
37  </body>
38  </html>
```

Code Explained

```
01  <!DOCTYPE html>
02  <html>
```

Lines 1 and 2 tell the browser that this document contains HTML (line 1), and when the HTML starts (line 2)

```
03  <head>
```

Line 3 begins the HEAD section of the document.

```
04      <style type="text/css">
05      * { font-family: Arial; }
06      label { width: 10em; float: left; }
07      input, textarea { width: 15em; }
08      .submit { margin-left: 13em; margin-top: 2em;}
09      </style>
```

Lines 4 - 9 contain styles to format the document . **Line 5** uses the * selector, which selects everything, then sets the default font to Arial. **Line 6** defines how labels shall look, **Line 7** how the input elements should look, and **Line 8** defines how the submit button should look.

```
11  </head>
12  <body>
```

Line 11 closes the HEAD area and **Line 12** begins the body area.

```
13  <form id="comments" method="get" action="">
14    <fieldset>
15      <legend>A simple form with no validation or messages</legend>
```

Line 13 starts the form. The important tag as far as jQuery is concerned is the id attribute, which in this case is 'comments'. We will use this **id** to tell jQuery which form to validate. **Line 14** begins a fieldset.

> The **fieldset** tag groups related elements in a form.

```
16    <div>
17      <label for="name">Name</label>
18      <input id="name" name="name" />
19    </div>
20    <div>
21      <label for="email" style="height: 1px">E-Mail</label>
22      <input id="email" name="email" />
23    </div>
24    <div>
25      <label for="url">URL (optional)</label>
26      <input id="url" name="url" class="url" value="" />
27    </div>
28    <div>
29      <label for="ccomment">Your comment</label>
30      <textarea id="ccomment" name="comment"></textarea>
31    </div>
32    <div>
33      <input class="submit" type="submit" value="Submit"/>
34    </div>
35    </fieldset>
```

Line 16 – 35 define the fields on the form. **Line 33** is the submit button.

```
36   </form>
37   </body>
38   </html>
```

Line 36 closes the form, **Line 37** closes the body, and **line 38** closes the html document.

A Form With jQuery Validation

I have also provided a version of this form that does have validation. The page is provided as '**validation.html**'

Code

```
01. <!DOCTYPE html>
02. <html>
03. <head>
04. <script src="jquery.min.js"></script>
05.  <script src="jquery.validate.js"></script>
06.
07.    <style type="text/css">
08.    * { font-family: Arial; }
09.    label { width: 10em; float: left; }
10.    label.error { float: none; color: red; padding-left: .5em; vertical-align: top; }
11.    div { clear: both; }
12.    input, textarea { width: 15em; }
13.    .submit { margin-left: 10em; }
14.    </style>
15.    <script type="text/javascript">
16.    jQuery(document).ready(function($){
17.      $("#comments").validate();
18.    });
19.    </script>
20. </head>
21. <body>
22.    <form id="comments" method="get" action="">
23.     <fieldset>
24.      <legend>A simple form with basic validation and messages</legend>
25.      <div>
26.       <label for="name">Name</label>
27.       <input id="name" name="name" class="required" minlength="2" />
28.      </div>
29.      <div>
30.       <label for="email">E-Mail</label>
31.       <input id="email" name="email" class="required email" />
```

```
32.    </div>
33.    <div>
34.      <label for="url">URL (optional)</label>
35.      <input id="url" name="url" class="url" value="" />
36.    </div>
37.    <div>
38.      <label for="comment">Your comment</label>
39.      <textarea id="comment" name="comment" class="required"></textarea>
40.    </div>
41.    <div>
42.      <input class="submit" type="submit" value="Submit"/>
43.    </div>
44.  </fieldset>
45.  </form>
46. </body>
47. </html>
```

Code Explained

I'll explain the changes to the form that will enable jQuery form validation.

```
04. <script src="jquery.min.js"></script>
05. <script src="jquery.validate.js"></script>
```

Line 4 adds the jQuery.min.js which is required by the jquery.validate.js, which is added on **Line 5**.

```
09.    label { width: 10em; float: left; }
10.    label.error { float: none; color: red; padding-left: .5em; vertical-align: top; }
11.    div { clear: both; }
```

Line 9 specifies the style elements of the label elements, while **Line 10** specifies the styling of the error messages.   (The error messages will be in red, and appear to the right of the field that triggered the error.)   Line 11 specifies that any DIV elements will not have any elements that float on either side of them. In other words, '**clear**' any elements that may float near me, and do this on **both** sides.

```
15.   <script type="text/javascript">
16.    jQuery(document).ready(function($){
17.      $("#comments").validate();
18.    });
19.  </script>
```

Lines 15 – 19 should seem familiar to us by now. They instruct jQuery what to do when the document is ready. In this case, we are telling jQuery to call the validate function against the selected element (the selected element being the form with id equal to 'comments').   The validate function is provided by the jQuery validation library, you may recall we added to the form in **line 5** with <script src="jquery.validate.js"></script>

How does the validate function know what values to validate and what values constitute valid data which values are invalid? Great question!   Line 27 is the first one provide an answer.

```
27.      <input id="name" name="name" class="required" minlength="2" />
```

Here we see that we have added the class='required' and minlength='2' to the input tag.   When the validation function examines the form, two levels of validation will be performed on name-- 1) that a a value has been provided (class='required') and that the value provided is at least two characters in length (minlength='2').

Line 31 provides an example of another type of validation

```
31.      <input id="email" name="email" class="required email" />
```

The class 'required email' means that a value must be provided, and that value must be a valid email address.

Here's some more:

```
34.      <label for="url">URL (optional)</label>
35.      <input id="url" name="url" class="url" value="" />
```

Line 34 and 35 provide the label and an input tag for the user to enter a URL. This value, if entered, must be a valid URL.   The attribute class ="url" sets this up. Had the field been required, the attribute would be class="required url"

7

jQuery UI Widgets: Dramatic Page Enhancements

Introduction

jQuery makes it easy to make your web forms shine, and look as if you are an awesome developer thanks to the jQuery UI library. The jQuery UI library is a separate, but related, library that is designed to work with jQuery.

UI stands for user-interface and the jQuery UI library provides user interface enhancements. These enhancements consist primarily of themes and widgets.

Themes

The jQuery UI provides a powerful theming engine. It allows you to create a theme for your site and apply it without too much fuss. There are two options, both of which are available from http://jqueryui.com/themeroller/

1. You can download a pre-defined theme from the jQuery gallery, or

2. You can create a custom theme on your own, using the 'roll your own' option.

Pre-defined themes

There are a number of pre-defined themes available that you can use freely. The nice thing about the pre-defined themes is that someone else has already gone to the trouble to make sure that the colors are compatible and that the whole thing looks good. If you don't really have a eye for design, and very few people do, you might just want to go for the pre-defined theme that you like the best.

To see how a theme will look, just click the image of the theme and all the controls on the screen will instantly update to use the selected theme.   To use a pre-defined theme, simply click the download button, as circled below

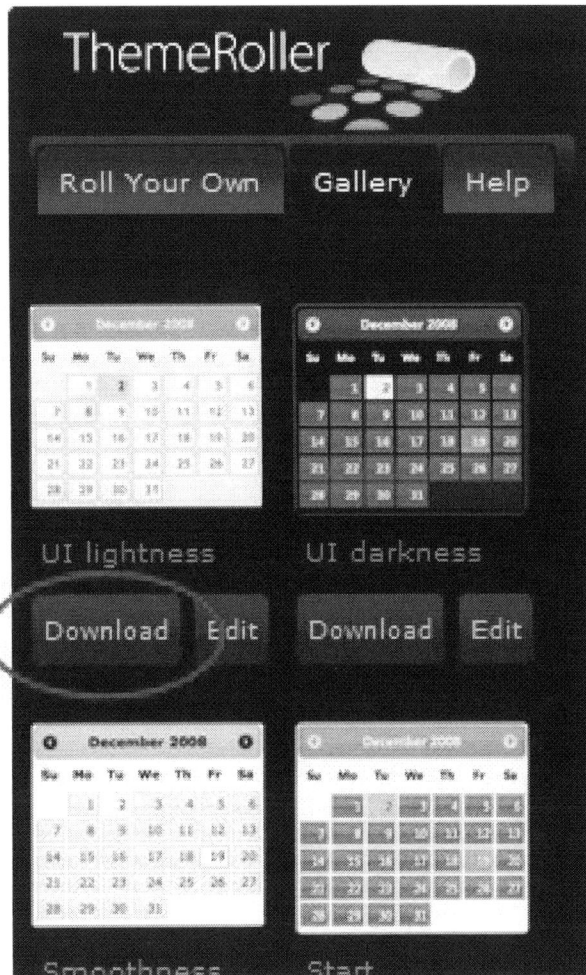

Custom Themes

One of the great features of the theme roller is that you can select a theme from the gallery and then customize it to your exact standards using the Edit button (you can also click the 'Roll Your Own' tab if you're feeling rebellious).

As you make changes to the various font and color options, you will see those changes reflected by the various widgets and animations on the right side.

This makes it easy to see what those changes will look like when applied to the various jQuery widgets.

Once you have a theme you love, you can download that theme to your computer. When you click the download button, you will be taken to the 'Download Builder' page where you can either download the entire jQuery library or pick and choose the items you require. This makes it very easy to get the smallest download possible, if that's your goal.

When you get the download, it will come as a a zipped file which contains the jQuery libraries, CSS files, and a demo page inside. Opening the demo file will how your theme will look and gives you some sample code to look at to see how it was applied. Here's a partial screen shot showing the sample file I download in researching this book:

Welcome to jQuery UI!

This page demonstrates the widgets you downloaded using th
ui-.custom.min.js), and css//jquery-ui-.custom.min.css which

You've downloaded components and a theme that are compa

YOUR COMPONENTS:

Accordion

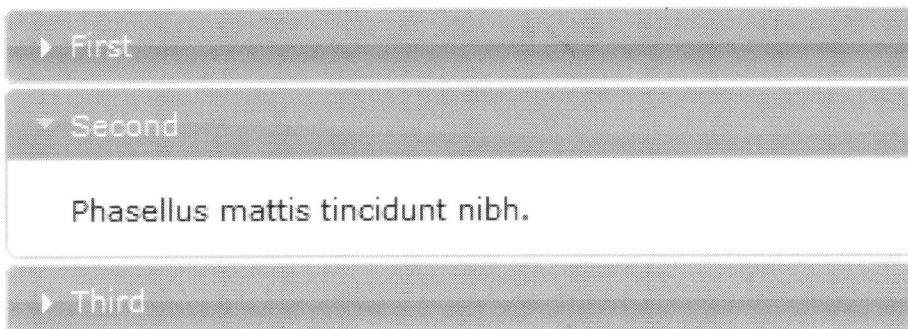

Autocomplete

Button

The CSS folder is where the theme is stored. There will be a CSS file and a folder with the images used by the widgets. Place these files on your website and reference the CSS file and you are ready to start adding widgets that will use your theme.

jQuery Widgets CDN

Again, both Microsoft and Google provide content delivery networks (CDN) for the jQuery UI. They also provide links to the CSS for themes in the gallery. You can find links to this below:

http://ajax.googleapis.com/ajax/libs/jqueryui/1.8.10/jquery-ui.js

Microsoft: http://www.asp.net/ajaxlibrary/CDNjQueryUI1910.ashx

Google: http://www.devcurry.com/2010/05/latest-jquery-and-jquery-ui-theme-links.html

Referencing jQuery UI

Now that you have your theme, it is time to start adding the jQuery UI to your web site. As stated above, you will need to reference these libraries and CSS files. In your <head> tag, you will add this:

```
<head>
    <script src="http://code.jquery.com/jquery-1.9.1.js"></script>
    <script src="http://code.jquery.com/ui/1.10.3/jquery-ui.js"></script>
    <script src="js/jquery-ui-1.10.3.custom.js"></script>
</head>
```

The first reference is the <script> reference for the jQuery library. The second <script> reference is for the jQuery UI library. The third and final <script> reference is for the jQuery UI CSS file that will add the theme. The first two <script> references are required to get the jQuery UI to work. You do not **have** to have a theme, but the UI will look bland without one.

Now that we have added the appropriate links for jQuery UI, we can now add some widgets and other items. Let us add a calendar widget. In the <head> tag, we add this:

```
<script>
     $(document).ready(function () {
        $("#datepicker").datepicker();
     });
</script>
```

In the body tag, we add this:

```
<p>Date: <input id="datepicker" type="text"></p>
```

What this code does is attaches a "datepicker" widget to the <input> box. Let's examine this more fully in the next section.

Date Picker

One common need on web forms is to ask the user to enter a date. In native HTML, the only option is to give the user a text field and hope that they input a valid date.

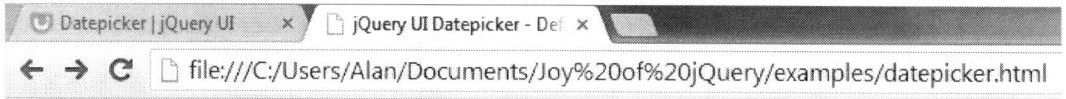

Joy of jQuery

When you would like to bring in your car for service?

Date: [_____]

The jQuery date field make it much easier for users to enter dates. The date picker modifies the behavior of a standard form input field. Simply focus on the input field (click, or use the tab key) and an interactive calendar will appear magically. Choose a date and the selected date is shown as the input's value.

Joy of jQuery

When you would like to bring in your car for service?

Date:

	September 2013					
Su	Mo	Tu	We	Th	Fr	Sa
1	2	3	4	5	6	7
8	9	10	11	12	13	14
15	16	17	18	19	20	21
22	23	24	25	26	27	28
29	30					

Code

```
01  <!doctype html>
02
03  <html lang="en">
04  <head>
05    <meta charset="utf-8" />
06    <title>jQuery UI Datepicker - Default functionality</title>
07    <link rel="stylesheet" href="jquery-ui.css" />
08    <script src="jquery-1.9.1.js"></script>
09    <script src="jquery-ui.js"></script>
10
11    <script>
12    $(function() {
13      $( "#datepicker" ).datepicker();
14    });
15    </script>
16  </head>
```

```
17  <body>
18   <h1>Joy of jQuery</h1>
19  <h2>When you would like to bring in your car for service?</h2>
20
21  <p>Date: <input type="text" id="datepicker" /></p>
22
23
24  </body>
25  </html>
```

Code Explained

```
01  <!doctype html>
02
03  <html lang="en">
04  <head>
05    <meta charset="utf-8" />
06    <title>jQuery UI Datepicker - Default functionality</title>
07    <link rel="stylesheet" href="jquery-ui.css" />
08    <script src="jquery-1.9.1.js"></script>
09    <script src="jquery-ui.js"></script>
```

Line 6 sets the title that appears in the browser. **Line 7** is the link to the jQuery UI style sheet (css) file. **Line 8** is the link to the jQuery library and **Line 9** is the link to the jQuery UI library. Lines 7, 8, and 9 will be common on any page that uses the jQuery UI.

```
11    <script>
12    $(function() {
13      $( "#datepicker" ).datepicker();
14    });
15    </script>
16  </head>
```

Line 11 starts a script block and **line 15** closes the script block. The script is what transforms the ordinary text input into the date picker. **Line 12** opens the short form of the jQuery document ready event. **Line 14** closes the block.

Line 13 is the the one that does all the work so we'll discuss it in some detail.

Remember, the basic jQuery syntax is **$(selector).action()**

The text to the left of the dot (highlighted in yellow below) selects the page element with the ID 'datepicker'.

$("#datepicker").datepicker();

The text to the right of the dot (highlighted in yellow below) tells jQuery to run the action 'datepicker' which is a function provided by the jQuery UI library.

$("#datepicker").datepicker();

```
17  <body>
18   <h1>Joy of jQuery</h1>
19  <h2>When you would like to bring in your car for service?</h2>
20
21  <p>Date: <input type="text" id="datepicker" /></p>
22
23
24  </body>
25  </html>
```

Lines 17 – 25 are pretty straight forward. We have a headline on **Line 18** and a subhead on **Line 19**.   **Line 21** has the text 'Date:' followed by an input box with the id of 'datapicker'. The id is critical because that is how jQuery selected this element to apply the date picker to.

Lines 24 and 25 close the HTML.

Auto-completing Text Fields

Sometimes the range of possible values makes radio buttons or selects inappropriate or just awkward. A great solution is to offer a text box and suggest values as the user begins to type. Google has shown the power of this techniques as it suggests search terms as you type them.

For instance, as I type the letters 'jq' into the search box, Google automatically suggests what I am really looking for, which of course is jquery!

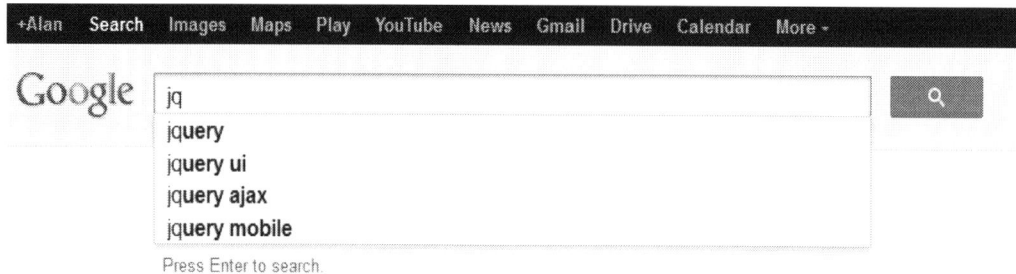

 How could we add such a cool feature into our application? jQuery makes it easy! Consider the following example

Code

```
1.    <!doctype html>
2.    <html lang="en">
3.    <head>
4.    <meta charset="utf-8" />
5.    <title>Joy of jQuery - Autocomplete</title>
6.     <link rel="stylesheet"
href="http://code.jquery.com/ui/1.10.3/themes/smoothness/jquery-ui.css" />
7.    <script src="http://code.jquery.com/jquery-1.9.1.js"></script>
8.    <script src="http://code.jquery.com/ui/1.10.3/jquery-ui.js"></script>
9.    <script>
10.   $(function() {
11.   var  carTypes = [
12.   "Audi",
13.   "BMW",
14.   "Buick",
```

```
15.    "Cadillac",
16.    "Chevrolet",
17.    "Chrysler",
18.    "Dodge",
19.    "Ferrari",
20.    "Fiat",
21.    "Fiskar",
22.    "GMC",
23.    "Honda",
24.    "Hyundai",
25.    "Infiniti",
26.    "Jaguar",
27.    "Jeep",
28.    "Kia",
29.    "Mazda",
30.    "Mercedes-Bens",
31.    "Mitsubishi",
32.    "Nissan",
33.    "Porsche",
34.    "Rolls-Royce",
35.    "Scion",
36.    "Suburu",
37.    "Toyota",
38.    "Volkswagon"
38.5   "Volvo"
39.    ];
40.    $( "#tags" ).autocomplete({
41.    source: carTypes
42.    });
43.    });
44.    </script>
45.    </head>
46.    <body>
47.    <h1>Joy of jQuery  - Sam's Used Cars</h1>
48.    <h2>What kind of car are you looking for?</h2>
49.    <div class="ui-widget">
50.    <label for="tags">Manufacturer: </label>
51.    <input id="tags" />
52.    </div>
```

```
53.    </body>
54.    </html>
```

Here's how the form will look when done.   A text box labeled 'Manufacturer' will automatically fill in car makes when you start to type.   This is so cool, you simply have to add it everywhere you can in your own web pages!

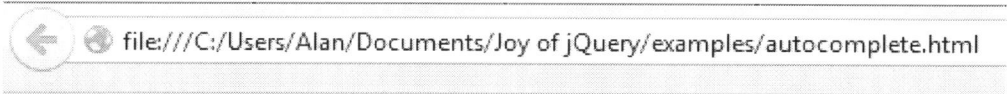

file:///C:/Users/Alan/Documents/Joy of jQuery/examples/autocomplete.html

Joy of jQuery - Sam's Used Cars

What kind of car are you looking for?

Manufacturer: Su

Mitsubishi
Suburu

Code Explained

```
01. <!doctype html>
02. <html lang="en">
03. <head>
04. <meta charset="utf-8" />
05. <title>Joy of jQuery - Autocomplete</title>
```

Lines 1 – 2 set up the document as html.   **Line 3** begins the head section. **Line 4** sets the character set and is probably not needed.   **Line 5** is the title of the page which appears at the top of the browser when the page is active.

```
06.  <link rel="stylesheet"
href="http://code.jquery.com/ui/1.10.3/themes/smoothness/jquery-ui.css" />
```

```
07. <script src="http://code.jquery.com/jquery-1.9.1.js"></script>
08. <script src="http://code.jquery.com/ui/1.10.3/jquery-ui.js"></script>
```

Line 6 is a link to the jQuery UI style sheet. See the chapter Introduction to CSS for an explanation of what a style sheet is.

Line 7 pulls down the base jQuery code while **line 8** pulls down the jQuery UI code.

```
09. <script>
10. $(function() {
11. var carTypes = [
12. "Audi",
...

37. "Toyota",
38. "Volkswagon"
39. ];
```

Line 9 begins a script block. **Line 10** is the start of the short version of the jQuery document ready event. **Line 11** declares a variable called carTypes that will be an array. The array is populated with automobile manufacturer names from **lines 12 to 38**. **Line 39** closes the variable declaration, and **Line 43** closes the script block.

```
40. $( "#tags" ).autocomplete({
41. source: carTypes
42. });
43. });
44. </script>
45. </head>
46. <body>
47.   <h1>Joy of jQuery  - Sam's Used Cars</h1>
48.   <h2>What kind of car are you looking for?</h2>
49.   <div class="ui-widget">
50.   <label for="tags">Manufacturer: </label>
51.   <input id="tags" />
52.   </div>
```

```
53.  </body>
54.  </html>
```

Line 40 is the start of the short version of the jQuery document ready event, which is closed on **Line 42**.

Remember, the basic jQuery syntax is **$(selector).action()**

As you can see, there is not much code required at all. A single jQuery statement (split across Lines 40 and 41) does all the work.

The text to the left of the dot (highlighted in yellow below) **selects** the page element with the ID 'tags'.

$("#tags").autocomplete({source: carTypes});

The text to the right of the dot (highlighted in yellow below) tells jQuery to run the **action** 'autocomplete' which is a function provided by the jQuery UI library.

$("#tags").autocomplete({source: carTypes});

Some jQuery actions require parameters and some do not. The Autocomplete widget takes a parameter specifying the source of the items that will be suggested. This makes sense because you want to be in control of the values that are suggested automatically.

jQuery UI Buttons

Buttons are extraordinarily easy to make with jQuery UI and they look much better than the standard HTML buttons. What's more, you can even style links to look like buttons.

Joy of jQuery

Examples of the jQuery button widget

A button element   A submit button   An anchor

Code

```
01.  <html>
02.  <head>
03.  <title>jQuery UI Button - Default functionality</title>
04.  <link rel="stylesheet" href="jquery-ui.css" />
05.  <link href="css/alan-theme/jquery-ui-1.10.3.custom.css" rel="stylesheet">
06.
07.  <script src="jquery-1.9.1.js"></script>
08.  <script src="jquery-ui.js"></script>
09.  <script>
10.  $(function() {
11.  $( "input[type=submit], a, button" )
12.  .button()
13.  });
14.  </script>
15.  </head>
16.  <body>
17.    <h1>Joy of jQuery</h1>
18.  <h2>Examples of the jQuery button widget</h2>
19.
20.  <button>A button element</button>
```

```
21.  <input type="submit" value="A submit button" />
22.  <a href="#">An anchor</a>
23.  </body>
24.  </html>
```

Code Explained

```
01.  <html>
02.  <head>
03.  <title>jQuery UI Button - Basic functionality</title>
04.  <link rel="stylesheet" href="jquery-ui.css" />
05.  <link href="css/alan-theme/jquery-ui-1.10.3.custom.css" rel="stylesheet">
06.
07.  <script src="jquery-1.9.1.js"></script>
08.  <script src="jquery-ui.js"></script>
```

Line 1 sets up the document as html. **Line 2** begins the head section. **Line 3** sets the document title which will be displayed at the top of the browser when the page is active.   **Line 4** is a link to the jQuery UI stylesheet. **Line 5** is a link to the optional theme stylesheet, which was described at the beginning of this chapter. Note that without this line, the buttons will still work but they look quite a bit duller, as shown below:

Joy of jQuery

Examples of the jQuery button widget

A button element   A submit button   An anchor

```
09.  <script>
10.  $(function() {
11.  $( "input[type=submit], a, button" )
```

```
12.  .button()
13.  });
14.  </script>
15.  </head>
```

Line 9 starts a script block which is closed on **Line 17.**   **Line 10** is the start of the short version of the jQuery document ready event, which is closed on **Line 13**.   When you get right to it, there is very much code at all   Like the last example, there is a single jQuery statement that does all the work.   Again, this clearly demonstrates the incredible power of the jQuery library.   A lot of code is happening behind the scenes.

Remember, the basic jQuery syntax is **$(selector).action()**

In this example we split the selector and the action onto two lines. **Line 11** is the selector and **line 12** is the action.   If we put it all on one line, then the text to the left of the dot (highlighted in yellow below) selects the page element that are input of type submit (input[type=submit],), anchor links (a), and buttons (button).

```
$( "input[type=submit], a, button" ).button();
```

The text to the right of the dot (highlighted in yellow below) tells jQuery to run the action 'button' which is a function provided by the jQuery UI library.

```
$( "input[type=submit], a, button" ).button();
```

Pretty simple, isn't it? The rest of the code is just simple HTML.

```
16.  <body>
17.    <h1>Joy of jQuery</h1>
18.    <h2>Examples of the jQuery button widget</h2>
```

```
19.
20.  <button>A button element</button>
21.  <input type="submit" value="A submit button" />
22.  <a href="#">An anchor</a>
23.  </body>
24.  </html>
```

Line 24 is the text for the headline *"Joy of jQuery"* and **line 25** is the subheading *"Examples of the jQuery button widget"*.

Lines 20 – 22 provide instances of the elements that we are transforming into jQuery buttons. **Line 23** closes the body tag opened on **Line 16** and **Line 24** closes the HTML tag opened on **Line 1.**

jQuery Menu

Menus are super easy in jQuery. Let's imagine that Sam's Used Cars would like its website to have a menu that makes it easy for customers to find their way around the site.   One way to do it would be to create an unordered list to serve as a navigator, as shown below.

- Buy a Car
- Sell a Car
    - Tow in
    - Drive in
- Finance
- Research a Car
- Service
    - Parts
        - OEM Parts
        - El Cheapo Parts
    - Repair
- Feedback

The jQuery menu widget can automatically transform a the simple unordered list shown above into a very cool and professional menu as shown below:

The Joy of jQuery: Sam's Used Cars

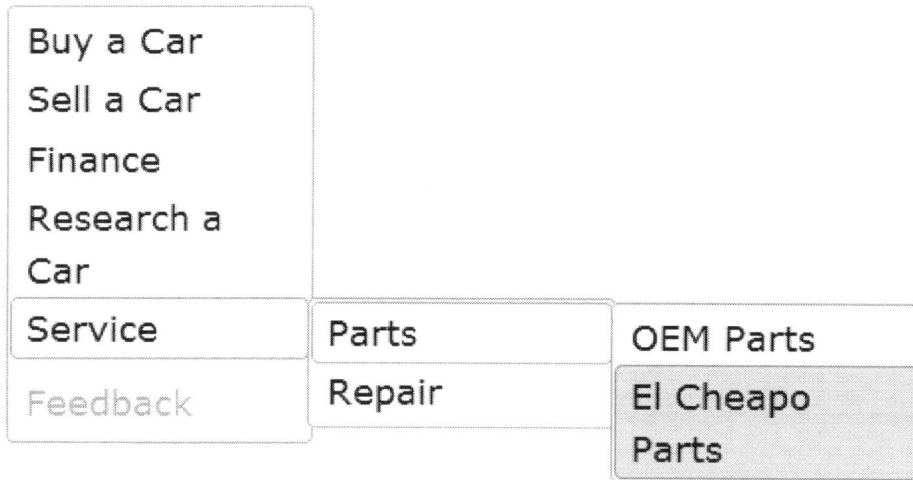

Buy a Car
Sell a Car
Finance
Research a Car
Service | Parts | OEM Parts
Feedback | Repair | El Cheapo Parts

Transforming a List into a Menu

How is this magical transformation achieved you ask? jQuery makes it **so simple** it is almost embarrassing!   But we don't need to tell anyone else how easy it is.   But the truth is that all you really need to do is add jQuery to the page and tell it which unordered list to transform into a menu.

For instance, imagine I have a list with the id attribute of menuCars, such as:

```
<ul id="menuCars">
<li><a href="buy.htm">Buy a Car</a></li>
<li>
<a href="sell.htm">Sell a Car</a>
....
```

To transform this list, I would add the following code:

```
<script>
$(function() {
$( "#menuCars" ).menu();
```

```
});
</script>
```

That's it. Sure you *can* tweak it with extra attributes, but you don't have to.
To play with this widget, check out the sample file menu.html or visit the
widget page at http://jqueryui.com/menu/#default

Example Menu Code

```html
<!doctype html>
<head>
<title>Joy of jQuery - jQuery UI Menu</title>
<link rel="stylesheet" href="jquery-ui.css" />
<script src="jquery-1.9.1.js"></script>
<script src="jquery-ui.js"></script>
<link rel="stylesheet" href="/resources/demos/style.css" />
<script>
$(function() {
$( "#menuCars" ).menu();
});
</script>
<style>
.ui-menu { width: 200px; }
</style>
</head>
<body>
<h1>The Joy of jQuery: Sam's Used Cars
</h1>
<ul id="menuCars">
<li><a href="#">Buy a Car</a></li>
<li>
<a href="#">Sell a Car</a>
<ul>
<li><a href="#">Tow in</a></li>
<li><a href="#">Drive in</a></li>
</ul>
</li>
<li><a href="#">Finance</a></li>
<li><a href="#">Research a Car</a></li>
```

```
<li>
<a href="#">Service</a>
<ul>
<li>
<a href="#">Parts</a>
<ul>
<li><a href="#">OEM Parts</a></li>
<li><a href="#">El Cheapo Parts</a></li>
</ul>
</li>
<li>
<a href="#">Repair</a>
</li>
</ul>
</li>
<li class="ui-state-disabled"><a href="#">Feedback</a></li>
</ul>
</body>
</html>
```

The astute reader may have noticed the list item titled 'Feedback' has the class *class="ui-state-disabled"*.   This prevents this item from being clicked. Clever, isn't it?   This is because Sam the used car dealer doesn't *really* want your feedback, he just wants your money.   :)

jQuery Progressbar

Often it is helpful to display to the user the status of an operation. In the case of Sam's Used Cars, perhaps Sam would like to user to have a sense of how close they are to having the customer's car ready. A progress bar is a great

The Joy of jQuery: Sam's Used Cars

Thank you for taking your car to Sam's Used Cars repair shop.

Your car is 37% repaired... In other words, we have successfully taken it apart.

way to show this visually.

A single jQuery statement does all the work.

```
<script>
$(function() {
$( "#progressbar" ).progressbar({value: 37});
});
</script>
```

Again, this clearly demonstrates the incredible power of the jQuery library. A lot of code is happening behind the scenes.

Remember, the basic jQuery syntax is **$(selector).action()**

The line doing the work is $("#progressbar").progressbar({value: 37}); In this example we are selecting a DIV with the ID of progressbar and telling jQuery to apply the progressbar function to it. The progressbar function takes a parameter of value to specify what percent of the bar should be filled in.

Here's a full example

Sample Code

```
01. <!doctype html>
02. <html lang="en">
03. <head>
04. <title>jQuery UI Progressbar - Default functionality</title>
05. <link rel="stylesheet"
href="http://code.jquery.com/ui/1.10.3/themes/smoothness/jquery-ui.css" />
06. <script src="http://code.jquery.com/jquery-1.9.1.js"></script>
07. <script src="http://code.jquery.com/ui/1.10.3/jquery-ui.js"></script>
08. <link rel="stylesheet" href="/resources/demos/style.css" />
09. <script>
10. $(function() {
11. $( "#progressbar" ).progressbar({
12. value: 37
13. });
14. });
15. </script>
16. </head>
17. <body>
18. <h1>The Joy of jQuery: Sam's Used Cars</h1>
19. <p>Thank you for taking your car to Sam's Used Cars repair shop.</p>
20. <p>Your car is 37% repaired... In other words, we have successfully taken it apart.</p>
21. <div id="progressbar"></div>
22. </body>
23. </html>
```

The relevant code for this widget can be found at line 11 and line 21.

jQuery Slider

A slider control is used to allow the user to select a value without having to type it in. Instead, the user simply drags a selector along a line. In the right situation, a slider can be very slick indeed, but you don't want to over do it.

If you've ever been shopping for a used car then you know that the first question you want answered as you approach a car is *how much does <u>this</u> car cost?* Conversely, the first question the salesperson approaching you wants to know is *how much can you spend?*

The salesperson will love the slider. A slider is an easy way for visitors to Sam's Used Cars website to specify how much they are willing to spend so that the appropriate cars can be displayed to the customer.   Here's how it could look:

Sam's Used Cars

Sam wants to put you into a new (used) car!

First, how much can you spend a month? ($25 increments): $225

The code to produce the slider is (again) pretty easy.   We create a div on the form and give it a unique id, for example 'slider'.   In the jQuery document ready event we select the div and apply the slider method to it.

The slider method takes a number of options, all of which are described at http://api.jqueryui.com/slider/

> Some common options to the slider widget include: value, min, max, and increment.

One important difference with this widget as compared with the ones shown so far is that the slider widget has an important **event** that we need to work with to make it useful. This is the slide event. The slide event is triggered every time the slider control moves. The value provided in the event as ui.value represents the value that the handle will have as a result of the current movement. Canceling the event will prevent the handle from moving and the handle will continue to have its previous value.

For example, as the user moves the slider around, Sam might want the value displayed as 'You're willing to pay $250 per month for your car' or something like that to make it clear to the user the value that they have just selected.

Code Sample

```
01.  <!doctype html>
02.  <html lang="en">
03.  <head>
04.  <meta charset="utf-8" />
05.  <title>Joy of jQuery - jQuery UI Slider</title>
06.  <link rel="stylesheet" href="jquery-ui.css" />
07.  <script src="jquery-1.9.1.js"></script>
08.  <script src="jquery-ui.js"></script>
09.  <link rel="stylesheet" href="/resources/demos/style.css" />
10.  <script>
11.  $(function() {
12.  $( "#slider" ).slider({
13.  value:200,
14.  min: 100,
15.  max: 500,
16.  step: 25,
17.  slide: function( event, ui ) {
18.  $( "#amount" ).val( "$" + ui.value );
19.  }
20.  });
21.  $( "#amount" ).val( "$" + $( "#slider" ).slider( "value" ) );
22.  });
23.  </script>
24.  </head>
25.  <body>
26.  <h1>
27.  <label for="amount">Sam's Used Cars</label></h1>
28.  <p>
29.  <label for="amount">Sam wants to put you into a new (used) car!</label></p>
30.  <p>
31.  <label for="amount">First, how much can you spend a month? ($25
increments):</label>
```

```
32.  <input type="text" id="amount" style="border: 0; color: green; font-weight: bold;" />
33.  </p>
34.  <div id="slider"></div>
35.
36.  <p>This example shows the slider snapping to specific increments, in this case
37.  $25 -- but you can change it to anything you want.</p>
38.
39.  </body>
40.  </html>
```

Code Explained

```
01.  <!doctype html>
02.  <html lang="en">
03.  <head>
04.  <meta charset="utf-8" />
05.  <title>Joy of jQuery - jQuery UI Slider</title>
06.  <link rel="stylesheet" href="jquery-ui.css" />
07.  <script src="jquery-1.9.1.js"></script>
08.  <script src="jquery-ui.js"></script>
09.  <link rel="stylesheet" href="/resources/demos/style.css" />
```

Lines 1 - 10 are common on all our widget examples and will no longer get a detailed explanation. They set up the page and reference the required jQuery files.

```
10.  <script>
11.  $(function() {
12.  $( "#slider" ).slider({
13.  value:200,
14.  min: 100,
15.  max: 500,
16.  step: 25,
17.  slide: function( event, ui ) {
18.  $( "#amount" ).val( "$" + ui.value );
19.  }
```

```
20. });
21. $( "#amount" ).val( "$" + $( "#slider" ).slider( "value" ) );
22. });
23. </script>
```

Lines 10 -23 are the most important ones in this example and will get the most attention. **Line 10** begins a script block. **Line 11** is the (now familiar) short version reference to the document onReady event. It means 'do the following things once the document is sufficiently loaded into the browser'.

Line 12 follows the standard syntax of selector/action to select the div with the id of 'slider' and apply the slider method to it. The slider method is defined in the jQuery library.

Remember, the basic jQuery syntax is **$(selector).action()**

The line doing the work is $("#slider").slider({value: 200, min:100, max:500, step:25 In this example we are selecting a DIV with the ID of slider and telling jQuery to transform it into a slider with an initial value of 200 (value:200), a minimum value of 100, a maximum value of 500, and the value incremented with each click as 25 (step:25).

So far so good, right?

The next part is a little tricky, so I'll repeat the code here so you don't have to scroll back up. Next we're going to concentrate on **lines 17 – 22**, but I'll show them in context.

```
12. $( "#slider" ).slider({
13. value:200,
14. min: 100,
15. max: 500,
16. step: 25,
```

```
17. slide: function( event, ui ) {
18. $( "#amount" ).val( "$" + ui.value );
19. }
20. });
21. $( "#amount" ).val( "$" + $( "#slider" ).slider( "value" ) );
22. });
24. </head>
```

Line 17 is different from the earlier options because instead of passing a simple value such as max:500, we are going to instead handle the slide event. An event is something that happens, such as when a button is clicked. In this case, the slide event occurs when the slider slides. We are going to pass the slide option a **function, as shown:**

```
slide: function( event, ui ) {
  $( "#amount" ).val( "$" + ui.value );
  }
```

In other words, when the slide **event** occurs, we are going to perform the following function:

```
$( "#amount" ).val( "$" + ui.value );
```

The astute reader (and by this I mean **you**) will notice that the function used to handle the slide event of the slider control itself uses jQuery!

> The function handling the slide event of the slider control follows the standard jQuery syntax of **$(selector).action()**

The function performs the following action: Select the thing with the ID of 'amount' and set its value to the dollar symbol and the current value of the slider control. I circled it in red below, so you can see what happens when the user drags the slider to the 225 mark.

Sam's Used Cars

Sam wants to put you into a new (used) car!

First, how much can you spend a month? ($25 increments): $225

The rest of the code is standard HTML and I'll skip explaining it. You can play with it using the included file **slider.html**.

jQuery Tabs

Tabs are a great way to group related information so that the page doesn't seem overwhelming to the user and to make it easier to find the information you are looking for.

In the case of a web site for a used car business, you might not want a long page full of information but rather to group related entries such as **Overview**, **Photographs**, and **Finance Calculator**, as shown below:

Sam's Used Cars

2013 Rolls-Royce Phantom Drophead Coupe Base - $507,800

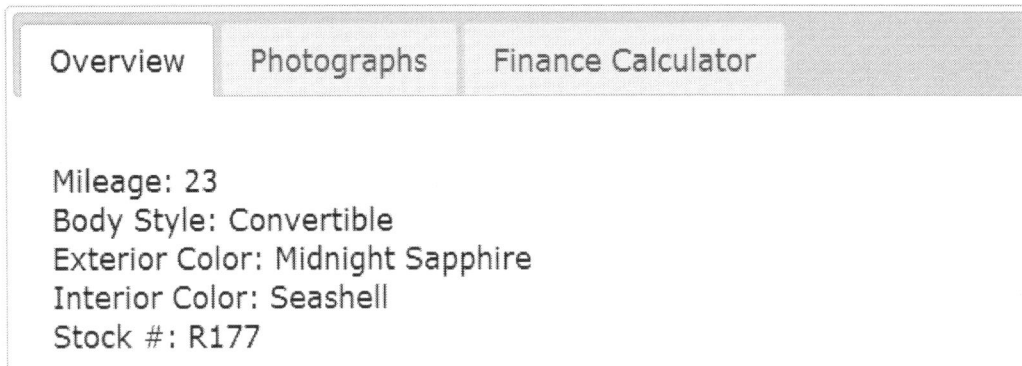

Overview	Photographs	Finance Calculator

Mileage: 23
Body Style: Convertible
Exterior Color: Midnight Sapphire
Interior Color: Seashell
Stock #: R177

The tab control works very much like the menu control. You start off with an unordered list, then transform it into something else with the magic of jQuery. Here's the relevant HTML snippet used to create the page shown above:

```
<div id="tabs">
<ul>
<li><a href="#tabs-1">Overview</a></li>
<li><a href="#tabs-2">Photographs</a></li>
<li><a href="#tabs-3">Finance Calculator</a></li>
```

```
</ul>
<div id="tabs-1">
<p>Mileage: 23<br>Body Style: Convertible<br>Exterior Color: Midnight
Sapphire<br>Interior Color: Seashell<br>Stock #: R177<br>
<br>Fuel: Gasoline<br>Engine: 6.8L V12 48V GDI DOHC<br>Transmission: 8-Speed
Automatic<br>Drivetrain: RWD<br>Doors: 2</p>
</div>
```

The jQuery code required is almost ridiculously simple:

```
$(function() {
$( "#tabs" ).tabs();
});
```

To put content inside the tab where you want it to go, create a div with an id
which matches the href target of the list. For example, in the code that
follows note that the string 'tabs-1' is common in both yellow highlights. This
is what links the tab to the content.

```
<div id="tabs">
<ul>
<li><a href="#tabs-1">Overview</a></li>
<li><a href="#tabs-2">Photographs</a></li>
<li><a href="#tabs-3">Finance Calculator</a></li>
</ul>
<div id="tabs-1">
<p>Mileage: 23<br>Body Style: Convertible<br>Exterior Color: Midnight
Sapphire<br>Interior Color: Seashell<br>Stock #: R177<br>
<br>Fuel: Gasoline<br>Engine: 6.8L V12 48V GDI DOHC<br>Transmission: 8-Speed
Automatic<br>Drivetrain: RWD<br>Doors: 2</p>
</div>
```

What we have done is specified that the tab with the label of Overview will
contain the content which is specified in the div with the id of 'tabs-1'. It
really doesn't matter what we call our tabs, as long as they match up.

Check out the sample file included as tabs.html.

Code

```
<!doctype html>
<html lang="en">
<head>
<meta charset="utf-8" />
<title>Joy of jQuery - UI Tabs</title>
<link rel="stylesheet" href="jquery-ui.css" />
<script src="jquery-1.9.1.js"></script>
<script src="jquery-ui.js"></script>
<link rel="stylesheet" href="/resources/demos/style.css" />
<script>
$(function() {
$( "#tabs" ).tabs();
});
</script>
</head>
<body>
<h1>Sam's Used Cars</h1>
<h2>2013 Rolls-Royce Phantom Drophead Coupe Base - $507,800
</h2>
<div id="tabs">
<ul>
<li><a href="#tabs-1">Overview</a></li>
<li><a href="#tabs-2">Photographs</a></li>
<li><a href="#tabs-3">Finance Calculator</a></li>
</ul>
<div id="tabs-1">
<p>Mileage: 23<br>Body Style: Convertible<br>Exterior Color: Midnight
Sapphire<br>Interior Color: Seashell<br>Stock #: R177<br>
<br>Fuel: Gasoline<br>Engine: 6.8L V12 48V GDI DOHC<br>Transmission: 8-Speed
Automatic<br>Drivetrain: RWD<br>Doors: 2</p>
</div>
<div id="tabs-2">
<p><img alt="Rolls Royce Interior" height="266" src="Rolls.jpg" width="400"></p>
</div>
<div id="tabs-3">
<p>Seriously.  If you have to ask, you can't afford this one. </p>
</div>
```

```
</div>
</body>
</html>
```

Other Widgets

Obviously, there are **many** more jQuery UI widgets than the few shown here--such as the official widgets of Accordian, Spinner and Tooltip--but they all work in a consistent way, which is $(selector).action()

> The basic jQuery syntax, even for UI widgets, is **$(selector).action()**

8

jQuery Mobile

Introduction

At the risk of stating the obvious, mobile devices are extremely popular and thus very important to web developers. jQuery Mobile is an HTML 5 based toolkit built on top of jQuery that makes it extremely easy to build web pages that are optimized for mobile users.

It looks great on iOS and Android, and other mobile devices. The nice thing is that jQuery Mobile looks great on all these devices and you don't need to write code for each specific device.

Getting Started

Links to jQuery Mobile CDN

Copy-and-Paste Snippet for CDN-hosted files (recommended):

```
<link rel="stylesheet" href="http://code.jquery.com/mobile/1.3.2/jquery.mobile-1.3.2.min.css" />
<script src="http://code.jquery.com/jquery-1.9.1.min.js"></script>
<script src="http://code.jquery.com/mobile/1.3.2/jquery.mobile-1.3.2.min.js"></script>
```

Hello (mobile) World!

Here's an example of a very basic jQuery Mobile page, in the tradition of the classic 'Hello World' example:

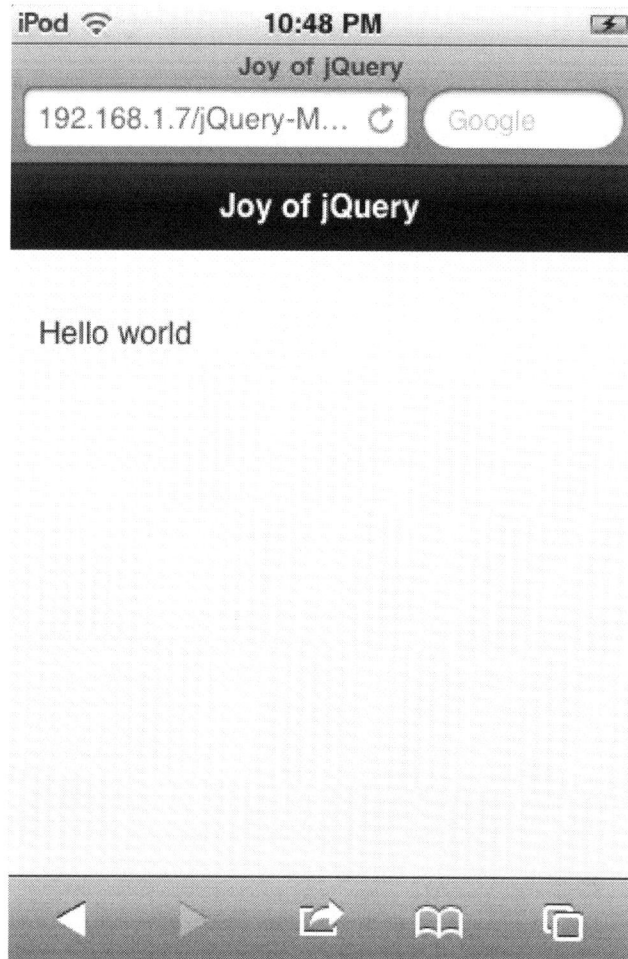

Hello (mobile) World Source Code

Here's the code that produced the above screen shot. You can find the source code for this file in the jQuery Mobile folder as **1-hello-mobile-world.html**

```
1.  <!DOCTYPE html>
2.  <html>
3.  <head>
4.    <title>Joy of jQuery</title>
5.    <meta name="viewport" content="width=device-width, initial-scale=1" />
6.    <meta http-equiv="content-type" content="text/html; charset=utf-8" />
7.    <link rel="stylesheet" href="http://code.jquery.com/mobile/1.3.2/jquery.mobile-1.3.2.min.css" />
8.    <script src="http://code.jquery.com/jquery-1.9.1.min.js"></script>
9.    <script src="http://code.jquery.com/mobile/1.3.2/jquery.mobile-1.3.2.min.js"></script>
10. </head>
11. <body>
12.
13. <div data-role="page">
14.
15.   <div data-role="header">
16.     <h1>Joy of jQuery</h1>
17.   </div> <!-- /header -->
18.
19.   <div data-role="content">
20.     <p>Hello world</p>
21.   </div> <!-- /content -->
22.
23. </div> <!-- /page -->
24.
25. </body>
26. </html>
```

The first thing to notice is on line 1 --   <!DOCTYPE html>. jQuery mobile is based on HTML 5 and that means that you have to declare the doc type. You'll also see a number of DIVs with various roles defined, such as data-role="page" or data=role="header".   This is how you define the various elements on a jQuery mobile page.   Let's look in more detail.

1. <!DOCTYPE html>
2. <html>
3. <head>
4.   <title>Joy of jQuery</title>
5.   <meta name="viewport" content="width=device-width, initial-scale=1" />

Line 1 specifies the document type,and this line is required for jQuery mobile applications.   **Line 2** begins the html, and **Line 3** begins the head section of the document.

Line 4 is the document title, and this would appear in the browsers title bar and is also used by search engines.   So far, we have entered only standard html.

Line 5 is new for us. It tells the browser that the "viewport" (the part of the page that is visible on the mobile device) should be as wide as the device width with an initial scale of 1.   In short, you can take this line as is for 99% of your jQuery mobile pages. Without this line, the mobile browser will try to scale the document and it will look bad.

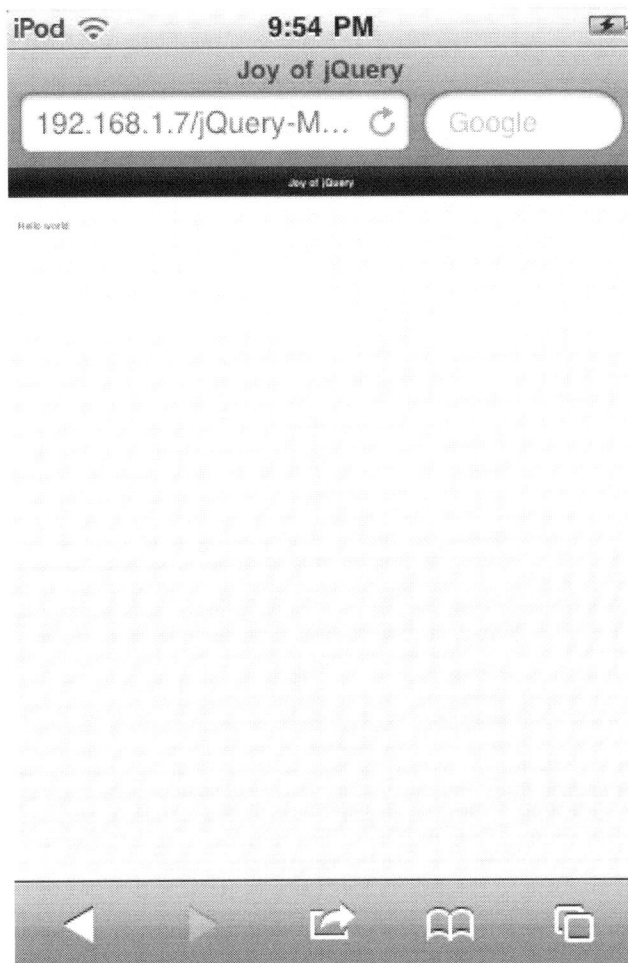

6.   <meta http-equiv="content-type" content="text/html; charset=utf-8" />
7.   <link rel="stylesheet" href="http://code.jquery.com/mobile/1.3.2/jquery.mobile-1.3.2.min.css" />
8.   <script src="http://code.jquery.com/jquery-1.9.1.min.js"></script>
9.   <script src="http://code.jquery.com/mobile/1.3.2/jquery.mobile-1.3.2.min.js"></script>

Line 6 is another one of those required ones.   jQuery Mobile likes to know the character set. Just put it in all your mobile pages, and don't worry about it.

Line 7 is a link to the jQuery mobile style sheet. **Line 8** is a reference to the jQuery library, and finally **line 9** is a reference to the jQuery mobile library. Note that you must include the jQuery mobile library *AFTER* you enter the jQuery library, because one relies on the other.

> You must enter the reference to jQuery mobile after referencing jQuery. jQuery mobile extends jQuery so jQuery must be loaded first in the document.

```
10. </head>
11. <body>
12.
13. <div data-role="page">
14.
15.    <div data-role="header">
16.       <h1>Joy of jQuery</h1>
17.    </div> <!-- /header -->
18.
19.    <div data-role="content">
20.       <p>Hello world</p>
21.    </div> <!-- /content -->
22.
23. </div> <!-- /page -->
24.
25. </body>
26. </html>
```

Line 13 is the start of a DIV that ends on **Line 23**.   Notice that the DIVs in the document all contain an attribute called data-role. The data-role tells jQuery mobile how the particular DIV should be formatted. The jQuery Mobile framework uses HTML5 data- attributes to allow for markup-based initialization and configuration of widgets.

There are many types of data roles, but in the interest of keeping this first page simple we have limited our data-roles to page, header, and content.

jQuery Mobile Theming

The default theme includes 5 swatches that are given letters (a, b, c, d, e) for quick reference. This makes things super easy. To make mapping of color swatches consistent across widgets, the jQuery team followed the convention that swatch "a" is the highest level of visual priority (black in our default theme), "b" is secondary level (blue) and "c" is the baseline level (gray) that we use by default in many situations, "d" for an alternate secondary level and "e" as an accent swatch.

Bar A - Link

Bar B - Link

Bar C - Link

Bar D - Link

Bar E - Link

Using a specific swatch is super easy. For instance, if I wanted to modify the *'hello mobile world'* example to use the "b" theme in the header bar, I would make the following code change:

```
<div data-role="header" data-theme="b">
```

You can put the data-theme element in any jQuery div with a data-role and it will be themed appropriately.   Thus it follows that to change the look of the content area one would do this:

```
<div data-role="content" data-theme="b">
```

Exercise

Try experimenting by putting the data-theme attribute to different sections of the page. You'll see that get different results depending where you apply it. See if you can get it to look like this:

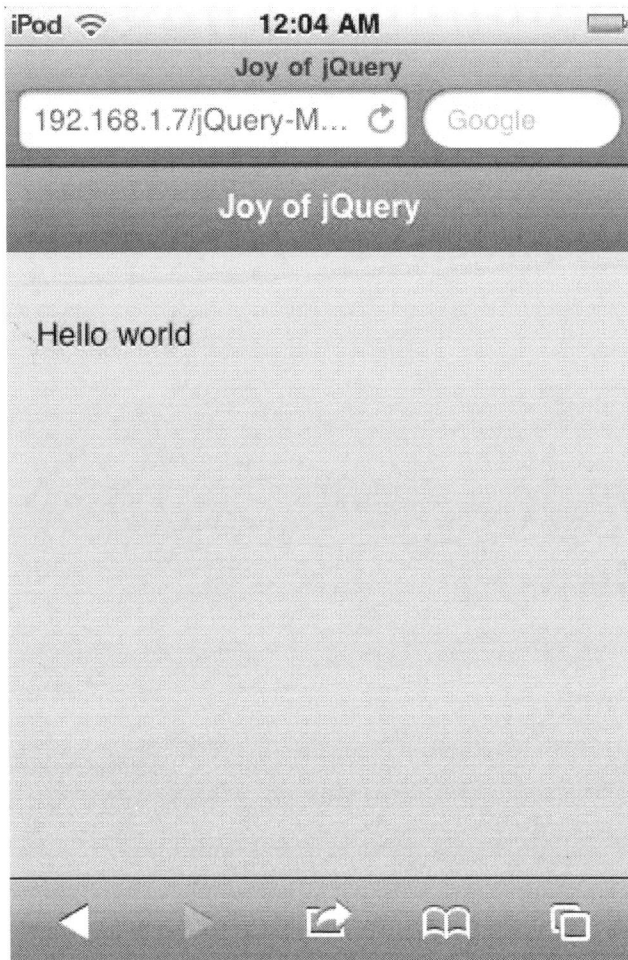

How to test your Mobile Pages

You may have noticed that examples used in the book all have a web address that starts with an IP address of 192.186.... That's because when I work on mobile web pages, I put them under the WAMP folder on my laptop computer. WAMP (for those of you who haven't read my 'Joy of PHP' book or worked with WAMP before, it's a super-easy (and free) web server you can install on just about any computer and it can host pages like this easily. Just Google 'download WAMP' and you'll find it.

My laptop is *not* accessible over the Internet, but it *is* accessible to other computers (and mobile devices) on the same local network (i.e., sharing the WIFI in my house).   So I just found the IP address of my laptop (on Windows choose Run, CMD, ipConfig) and entered that address into the address bar on my iPod.

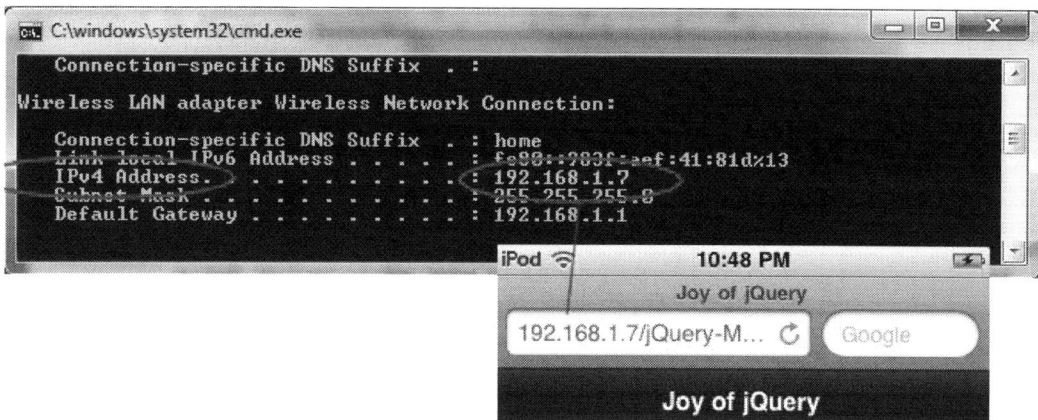

No doubt a similar method exists for those readers using the Apple platform, but that's the concept.

A More Advanced Example with UI elements and multiple pages

OK, so we've mastered 'hello world' and it's time to step things up a bit. Next we'll be building a page for *Sam's Used Car* site to allow mobile users to browse the car lot as easily as regular visitors can. This example can be found in the source code as **2-Sam-Mobile.html**

The page we're building will look like this:

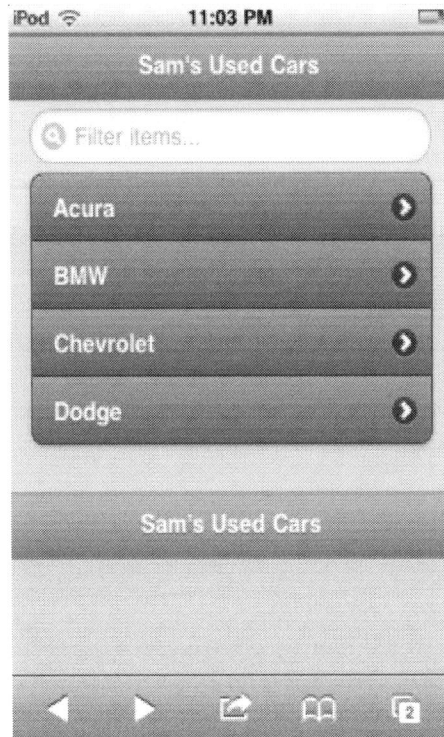

clicking on a link will slide in a new page, such as

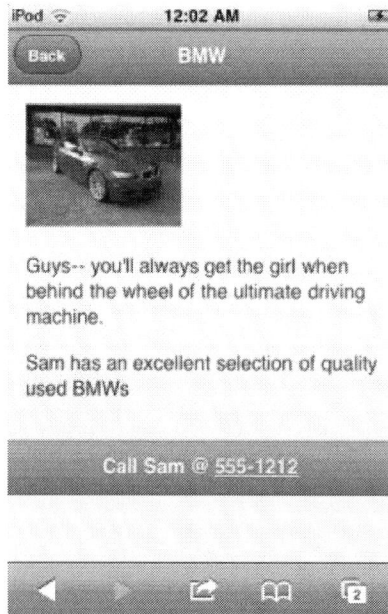

Or the following page, which is themed using the 'e' theme

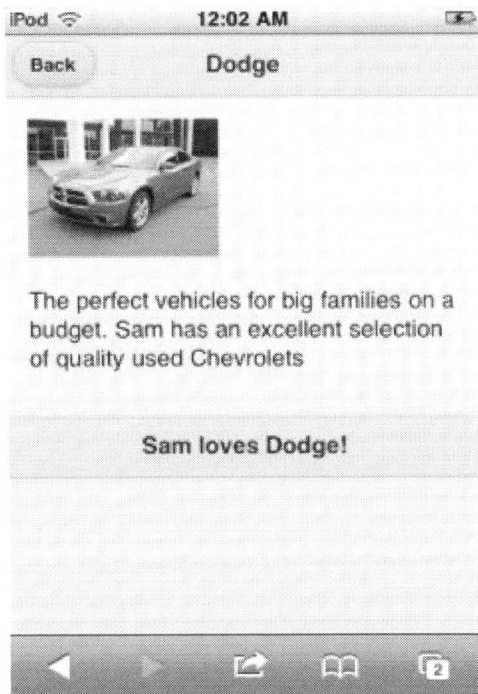

Code for Sam's Used Cars – Mobile Site

This code may seem long, but it really isn't conceptually difficult. Don't be intimidated by the length. I'll explain it, and you'll get it!

Code

```
1.  <!DOCTYPE html>
2.  <html>
3.  <head>
4.     <title>Joy of jQuery</title>
5.      <meta name="viewport" content="width=device-width, initial-scale=1" />
6.    <meta http-equiv="content-type" content="text/html; charset=utf-8" />
7.    <link rel="stylesheet" href="http://code.jquery.com/mobile/1.3.2/jquery.mobile-1.3.2.min.css" />
8.    <script src="http://code.jquery.com/jquery-1.9.1.min.js"></script>
```

```
9.   <script src="http://code.jquery.com/mobile/1.3.2/jquery.mobile-1.3.2.min.js"></script>
10.
11.
12.
13.   <!-- to avoid header text from being
14.      truncated overwrite the margin -->
15.   <style type="text/css">
16.    .ui-header .ui-title {
17.     margin-right: 10%;
18.     margin-left: 10%;
19.    }
20.   </style>
21.  </head>
22.  <body>
23.
24.  <div data-role="page" id="mainPage" data-theme="b">
25.
26.    <div data-role="header" data-theme="b">
27.
28.      <h4>Sam's Used Cars</h4>
29.    </div>
30.    <div data-role="content">
31.     <ul data-role="listview" data-inset="true" data-filter="true">
32.      <li><a href="#Acura" data-transition="slide">Acura</a></li>
33.      <li><a href="#BMW" data-transition="slide">BMW</a></li>
34.      <li><a href="#Chevy" data-transition="slide">Chevrolet</a></li>
35.      <li><a href="#Dodge" data-transition="slide">Dodge</a></li>
36.     </ul>
37.    </div>
38.    <div data-role="footer" data-theme="b">
39.
40.      <h4>Sam's Used Cars</h4>
41.    </div>
42.  </div>
43.
44.  <div data-role="page" id="Acura">
45.    <div data-role="header" data-theme="b">
46.
47.     <a data-rel="back" data-direction="reverse" href="#mainPage">Back</a>
```

```
48.    <h1>Acura</h1>
49.    </div>
50.    <div data-role="content">
51.    <img border="0" src="img/acura.jpg" />
52.     <p>Sam just got a new shipment of Acuras for you!  These babies are going fast so
don't delay...</p>
53.    </div>
54.    <div data-role="footer" data-theme="b">
55.
56.     <h4>Call Sam now!</h4>
57.    </div>
58.  </div>
59.
60.
61.  <div data-role="page" id="BMW">
62.    <div data-role="header" data-theme="b">
63.
64.     <a data-rel="back" data-direction="reverse" href="#mainPage">Back</a>
65.     <h1>BMW</h1>
66.    </div>
67.    <div data-role="content">
68.     <img border="0" src="img/bmw.jpg"/>
69.    <p>Guys-- you'll always get the girl when behind the wheel of the ultimate driving
machine.</p><p> Sam has an excellent selection of quality used BMWs</p>
70.    </div>
71.    <div data-role="footer" data-theme="b">
72.     <h4>Call Sam @ 555-1212</h4>
73.    </div>
74.  </div>
75.
76.  <div data-role="page" id="Chevy">
77.    <div data-role="header">
78.     <a data-rel="back" data-direction="reverse" href="#mainPage">Back</a>
79.     <h1>Chevrolet</h1>
80.    </div>
81.    <div data-role="content">
82.     <img border="0" src="img/chevy.jpg"/>
83.      <p>The perfect vehicles for big families on a budget. Sam has an excellent selection
of quality used Chevrolets</p>
```

```
84.
85.    </div>
86.    <div data-role="footer">
87.      <h4>Call Sam Today!</h4>
88.    </div>
89.  </div>
90.
91.  <div data-role="page" id="Dodge" data-theme="e">
92.
93.    <div data-role="header" data-theme="e">
94.
95.     <a data-rel="back" data-direction="reverse" href="#mainPage">Back</a>
96.      <h1>Dodge</h1>
97.    </div>
98.    <div data-role="content">
99.      <img border="0" src="img/dodge.jpg" />
100.       <p>The perfect vehicles for big families on a budget. Sam has an excellent selection
of quality used Chevrolets</p>
101.
102.    </div>
103.    <div data-role="footer" data-theme="e">
104.      <h4>Sam loves Dodge!</h4>
105.  </div>
106.  </div>
107.  </body>
108.  </html>
```

Code Explained

Although when you look at this 'web site' it seems like it is made up of several independent pages, it is really all just a single page with sub-pages. That's why it seems so long. But if you can understand how one of the sub pages work, then you'll understand how the whole thing works.

Here's the subset of code that produces the main page. We're showing lines 24 – 42 here:

```
<div data-role="page" id="mainPage" data-theme="b">
<div data-role="header" data-theme="b">
      <h4>Sam's Used Cars</h4>
</div>

<div data-role="content">
  <ul data-role="listview" data-inset="true" data-filter="true">
   <li><a href="#Acura" data-transition="slide">Acura</a> </li>
   <li><a href="#BMW" data-transition="slide">BMW</a> </li>
   <li><a href="#Chevy" data-transition="slide">Chevrolet</a> </li>
   <li><a href="#Dodge" data-transition="slide">Dodge</a></li>
    </ul>
</div>

<div data-role="footer" data-theme="b">
      <h4>Sam's Used Cars</h4>
  </div>
</div>
```

You have a DIV that with the data-role of **page**. That means that the content of this DIV will define a single page when rendered on a mobile device.   It's the first DIV with this element, so it's the first page that is display.   Next comes a DIV with the data-role of **header**. This is the headline at the top of the page. The next DIV has the data-role of **content**, and of course that's where the main content of the page goes.   Inside the content area is an unordered list <ul> with four list items: Acura, BMW, Chevy, and Dodge. jQuery transforms this simple unordered list into a touch friendly group of buttons. Finally, there is a DIV with the data-role of **footer**, which defines what goes onto the bottom of the page.

Here's an image to help explains how this all works:

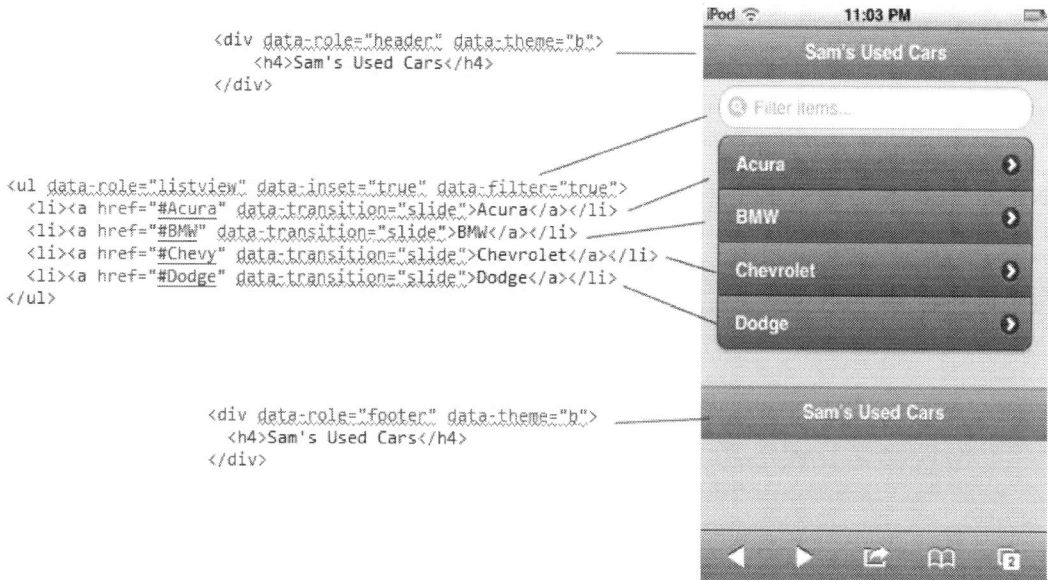

```
<div data-role="header" data-theme="b">
    <h4>Sam's Used Cars</h4>
</div>

<ul data-role="listview" data-inset="true" data-filter="true">
  <li><a href="#Acura" data-transition="slide">Acura</a></li>
  <li><a href="#BMW" data-transition="slide">BMW</a></li>
  <li><a href="#Chevy" data-transition="slide">Chevrolet</a></li>
  <li><a href="#Dodge" data-transition="slide">Dodge</a></li>
</ul>

<div data-role="footer" data-theme="b">
    <h4>Sam's Used Cars</h4>
</div>
```

Clicking on any of the links specified in the unordered list (in other words clicking on any of the **big shiny buttons** from a mobile device) will take you to a new page.

How does that part work? This is basic HTML in that if we look at one of the links such as:

```
<li><a href="#BMW" data-transition="slide">BMW</a></li>
```

You see that there is an anchor link with the HREF set to '#something'. In HTML when the HREF destination is preceded by the pound symbol (#) that takes you to an element on the **same page** labeled with that identifier. In our case, that 'other element' will be a DIV with the ID of BMW, as shown below:

```
<div data-role="page" id="BMW">
```

```
<div data-role="header" data-theme="b">
    <a data-rel="back" data-direction="reverse" href="#mainPage">Back</a>
  <h1>BMW</h1>
</div>
<div data-role="content">
  <img border="0" src="img/bmw.jpg"/>
  <p>Guys-- you'll always get the girl when behind the wheel of the ultimate driving
machine.</p>
  <p> Sam has an excellent selection of quality used BMWs.</p>
</div>
<div data-role="footer" data-theme="b">
  <h4>Call Sam @ 555-1212</h4>
</div>
</div>
```

You'll see that the BMW DIV has the same basic elements at the main page with a header, footer, and content area.   The only elements that are new is the inclusion of an image, and the inclusion of the back button. The back button is included inside the header DIV and is implemented as follows:

```
<a data-rel="back" data-direction="reverse" href="#mainPage">Back</a>
```

All the other pages work the same way too.

9

jQuery AJAX

AJAX is a method of requesting data from a server and updating *selected* parts of the current page with the server's response. Once you have experienced it you will see why AJAX is such a powerful technique. This means that users can make a selection or click on an item on your page and the page will respond by updating to reflect the selection without having to reload the whole page as is the case with traditional server-side scripting.

AJAX is a much better method than reloading a whole page when information changes because it makes a page seem more responsive and dynamic.

The good news is that jQuery has this topic covered too! You'll learn in this chapter that it is very easy to load any static or dynamic data using jQuery AJAX. Note that the example givens here are intended get you started. jQuery AJAX is a very rich topic all on its own.

Basic AJAX Syntax - Get/Post

The jQuery get() and post() methods are used to request data from the server with an HTTP GET or POST request.

GET vs. POST

- GET requests data **from** a specified resource.

- POST submits data **to** a specified resource to be processed.

GET is used for getting data from a server.   Note that this method may return cached data, depending on the server or browser settings.

POST can also be used to get data from the server. However, there are two major differences when contrasted with GET.   First, the POST method never returns cached data, and second, it can be used to send data along with the request. In other words, the POST command can submit a form and send back the results.

jQuery $.get() Method

The $.get() method requests data from the server using an HTTP GET request. Here is the syntax for get() method:

```
$.get(URL, callback);
```

The *required* URL parameter specifies the URL you wish to request (get) and the *optional* callback parameter is the name of a function that will be executed if the request succeeds.

jQuery $.get() Example

The following example uses the $.get() method to retrieve data from a file on the server:

```
$("button").click(function(){
  $.get("todays_deal.php",function(data,status){
   alert("Data: " + data + "\nStatus: " + status);
  });
});
```

The first parameter of $.get() is the URL we wish to request ("todays_deal.php").

The second parameter is a callback function. A "callback function" is a fancy way of saying that this is the function that will be run if the **get** succeeds. The callback function itself has parameters which are given values by jQuery if the **get** succeeds. The first parameter will hold the *content* of the page requested, and the second callback parameter will hold the *status* of the request. At first I assumed that the value of the status parameter could only be "success" because, by definition, the function is only called if the get succeeds. However, a little Googling turned up other possible values as well such as "notmodified", "error", "timeout", or "parsererror".

By the way, the PHP file called above ("todays_deal.php") looks like this:

```
<?php  echo ("Today only-- Sam has an awesome deal for you!");  ?>
```

jQuery $.post() Method

The $.post() method requests data from the server using an HTTP POST request.

Here is the syntax for post() method:

```
$.post(URL,data,callback);
```

As with **get**, the *required* URL parameter specifies the URL you wish to request.

The *optional* data parameter specifies some data to send along with the request.

As with **get**, the *optional* callback parameter is the name of a function that will be executed if the request succeeds.

jQuery $.post() Example

The following example uses the $.post() method to send some data along with a request to retrieve data from a server. Since this particular example relies on a php-based server-side script, I have posted it on http://www.joyofphp.com/ajaxpost.html so you can try it out.

```
01.  <html>
02.  <head>
03.  <title>Joy of jQuery - Simple Ajax POST Example</title>
04.    <link rel="stylesheet" href="jquery-ui.css" />
05.  <script src="jquery-1.9.1.js"></script>
06.  <script>
07.  $(document).ready(function(){
08.    $("button").click(function(){
09.    var Make = $('input[type="radio"]:checked').val();
10.       $.post("response.php",
11.    {
12.      Make: Make
13.       },
14.      function(data,status){
15.      // alert("Data: " + data + "\nStatus: " + status);
16.        $("#deal").html(data);
17.
18.     });
19.    });
20.  });
21.  </script>
22.  </head>
23.  <body>
24.  <h1>Sam's Used Cars</h1>
25.  <p>Sam wants to put you into a new (used) car!  Click on the button to learn about
```

today's special:</p>
```
26.  <p>
27.  <form method="post">
28.  <input type="radio" name="Make" value="Ford">Ford<br>
29.  <input type="radio" name="Make" value="Dodge">Dodge<br>
30.  <input type="radio" name="Make" value="Honda">Honda<br>
31.
32.  </form>
33.  </p>
34.    <div id="deal" style="background-color:silver;">
35.        Today's Special
36.    </div>
37.  <br>
38.  <button>Send an HTTP POST request to a page and get the result back</button>
39.
40.  </body>
41.  </html>ctions-in Client Side JavaScripting, so only your computer will see or process
your data input/output.
```

The first parameter of $.post() is the URL we wish to request ("response.php").

Then we pass in some data to send along with the request (Make).

The PHP script in "response.php" reads the parameters, processes them, and returns a result.

The third parameter is a callback function. The first callback parameter holds the content of the page requested, and the second callback parameter holds the status of the request.

Tip: Here is how the PHP file looks like ("demo_test_post.asp"):

```
<?php
$Make = $_POST['Make'] ;
$Day = date("l");

switch ($Make ) {
```

```
  case "Dodge":
    echo "<h1>Dodge</h1>";
     echo "<p>The perfect vehicles for  families on a budget. $Day is Dodge day at Sam's
Used Cars.</p>";
     break;
  case "Ford":
    echo "<h1>Ford</h1>";
    echo "<p>The Ford Explorer is America's Favorite SUV. $Day is Ford day at Sam's Used
Cars. </p>";
     break;
  case "Honda":
    echo "<h1>Honda</h1>";
    echo "<p>$Day is Honda day at Sam's Used Cars.  Come on down...</p>";
       break;
  default:
      echo "<h1>$Make</h1>";
      echo "<p>$Day is your lucky day at Sam's Used Cars.  If we don't have a $Make we'll
find one for you!</p>";
       break;
}
 ?>
```

Alternate AJAX Syntax - Load

Load is similar to Get but adds functionality which allows you to define where
in the document the returned data should go. Therefore the load command is
really only a good fit for those times when you know that what you'll get back
is a snippet of well-formed HTML which you want to put someplace in your
document.

The load command is a method which is associated with a particular jQuery-
wrapped element which you first select using a jQuery selector.   The pattern
would be similar to:

```
$('#divWantingContent').load(...)
```

As an aside, it should be noted that the get(), post(), and load() commands
are really just "wrappers" for the more complicated (but more flexible) generic

$.ajax() command. In other words, when you call the **get** command what is *really* happening is that the .ajax() command is being called with all the parameters filled in for you automatically.   We are not going to cover the more generic .ajax() methods in this book, but if you find that neither get, post, or load do exactly what you need it is certainly good to know that jQuery provides even more flexible methods than these.

Here is the syntax for load() method:

```
[selector].load( URL, [data], [callback] );
```

Here is a description of the parameters:

URL: The URL of the server-side resource to which the request is sent. It could be a CGI, ASP, JSP, or PHP script which generates data dynamically or out of a database.

data: This optional parameter represents an object whose properties are serialized into properly encoded parameters to be passed to the request. If specified, the request is made using the POST method. If omitted, the GET method is used.

callback: The function which will be executed after the response data has been loaded into the elements of the matched set. The first parameter passed to this function is the response text received from the server and second parameter is the status code.

A Basic Example: Loading Simple Data

Let's start with a basic example. Imagine that Sam the used car dealer wants to have a page on his web site that reveals the "deal of the day" when visitors click a button. The page is set up with a div with the id of 'deal' which for convenience has a gray background.

Under the div is a button labeled 'Today's Special'.   When you click the button, the contents of the deal div will be replaced with the content of a separate HTML that contains the details of the deal.

Sam's Used Cars

Sam wants to put you into a new (used) car!   Click on the button to learn about today's special:

Today's Special

[Today's Special]

Clicking the button will reveal the deal of the day, such as:

Sam's Used Cars

Sam wants to put you into a new (used) car!   Click on the button to learn about today's special:

Dodge

The perfect vehicles for big families on a budget. Sam has an excellent selection of quality used Chevrolets

[Today's Special]

Code – ajax1.html

```
01.    <html>
02.    <head>
03.    <title>Joy of jQuery - Simple Ajax Example</title>
04.      <link rel="stylesheet" href="jquery-ui.css" />
05.    <script src="jquery-1.9.1.js"></script>
06.      <script type="text/javascript" language="javascript">
07.      $(document).ready(function() {
08.        $("#driver").click(function(event){
09.          $('#deal').load('result.html');
10.        });
11.      });
12.      </script>
13.    </head>
14.    <body>
15.    <h1>Sam's Used Cars</h1
16.    <p>Sam wants to put you into a new (used) car!   Click on the button to
learn about
         today's special:</p>
17.      <div id="deal" style="background-color:silver;">
18.        Today's Special
19.      </div>
20.      <br><input type="button" id="driver" value="Today's Special" />
21.    </body>
22.    </html>
```

When the button is clicked, the code that is loaded into the deal div is as follows:

Code – Result.html

```
<h1>Dodge</h1>
   <img border="0" src="img/dodge.jpg" />
    <p>The perfect vehicles for big families on a budget. Sam has an excellent selection of
quality used Chevrolets</p>
```

Code Explained

The part of the AJAX code that does the work is shown below

```
06.    <script type="text/javascript" language="javascript">
07.     $(document).ready(function() {
08.       $("#driver").click(function(event){
09.         $('#deal').load('result.html');
10.       });
11.     });
12.    </script>
```

Line 7 starts the familiar OnReady event. It states that when the document ready, attach a function to the click event of the item with the ID of 'driver' (this is the button).   This happens in **line 8.**

The function that will attached is specified in **line 9** → $ ('#deal').load('result.html');

Here is the simple syntax for load() method:

[selector].load(URL, [data], [callback]);

In this case we are only using the first parameter: *URL*.   What **line 9** does is select the div with the id of deal, and replace the HTML inside the div with the results of the URL that was loaded.

A More Advanced Example: Loading Data and Executing a Function

The optional callback parameter specifies a function that will run when the load() method is completed. The callback function can take three parameters:

- responseText - contains the text returned if the load succeeds

- statusText - contains the status of the call
- xhr - contains the XMLHttpRequest object

The following example modifies our earlier example to display an alert box after the load() method completes. If the load() method has succeed, it displays "External content loaded successfully!", and if it fails it displays an error message.

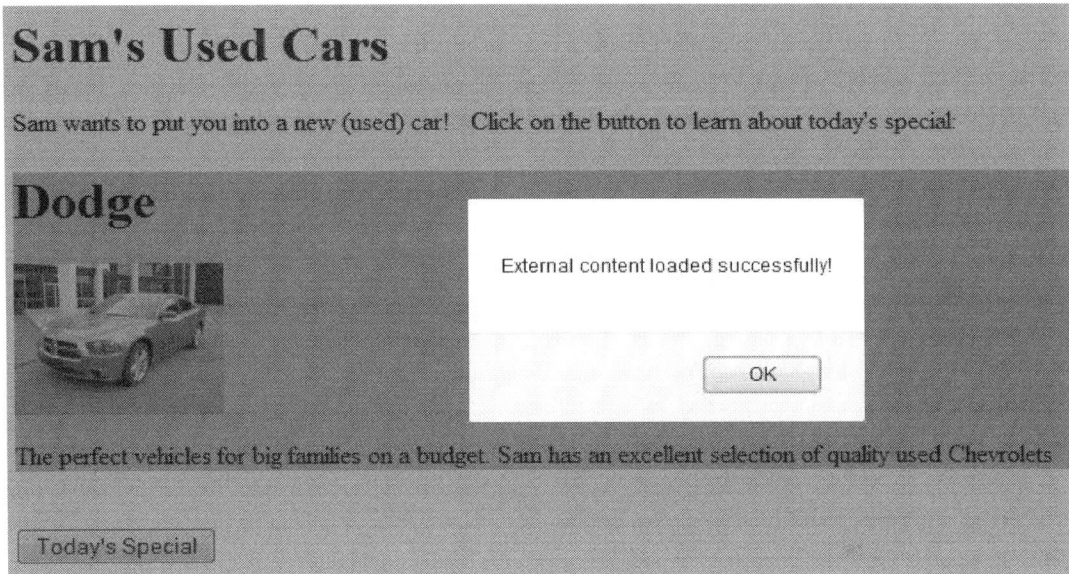

Old Code
| ```
$(document).ready(function() {
    $("#driver").click(function(event){
        $('#deal').load('result.html');
    });
});
``` |
| **New Code** |
| ```
$(document).ready(function() {
  $("#driver").click(function(){
        $("#deal").load("result.html",function(responseTxt,statusTxt,xhr){
          if(statusTxt=="success")
           alert("External content loaded successfully!");
          if(statusTxt=="error")
            alert("Error: "+xhr.status+": "+xhr.statusText);
                 });
        });
    });
``` |

Code – ajax2.html

```
$<html>
<head>
<title>Joy of jQuery - Simple Ajax Example</title>
 <link rel="stylesheet" href="jquery-ui.css" />
<script src="jquery-1.9.1.js"></script>

 <script type="text/javascript" language="javascript">
  $(document).ready(function() {
   $("#driver").click(function(){
        $("#deal").load("result.html",function(responseTxt,statusTxt,xhr){
          if(statusTxt=="success")
           alert("External content loaded successfully!");
          if(statusTxt=="error")
            alert("Error: "+xhr.status+": "+xhr.statusText);
```

```
                   });
            });
      });
   </script>
</head>
<body>
<h1>Sam's Used Cars</h1>
<p>Sam wants to put you into a new (used) car!   Click on the button to learn
about today's special:</p>
   <div id="deal" style="background-color:silver;">
       Today's Special
   </div>
   <br><input type="button" id="driver" value="Today's Special" />
</body>
</html>
```

Crossing Domains

You may have noticed that these examples load their dynamic content from
the same domain (or when running locally, the same folder).   Most browsers
prevent scripts from loading content into the current page from other
domains. As your mom used to say, 'this is for your own good!'.   The idea is
to prevent cross-domain scripts from loading malware into the current web
page of an unsuspecting user.

If you really need to pull data from another domain, investigate the jQuery
.ajax API documentation. There are **limited** cases where you *can* cross
domain, but this is beyond the scope of the book. For this, search for the
property **crossDomain** which you can find at
http://api.jquery.com/jQuery.ajax/ to learn more.

10

jQuery Animation

Of the many things that jQuery makes easy, animation is the most visible, and arguably one of the most fun. Just remember not to overdo it on your own web pages. Use animation where it makes sense, and not just for the sake of having animation everywhere.

jQuery hide(), show(), and toggle()

With jQuery, you can hide and show HTML elements with the hide() and show() methods:

Hide

```
$("#hide").click(function(){
  $("p.first()").hide();
});
```

Show

```
$("#show").click(function(){
  $("p.first()").show();
});
```

Syntax

```
$(selector).hide(speed,callback);
$(selector).show(speed,callback);
```

The optional speed **parameter** specifies the speed of the transition from one state to another and can take the values of "slow", "fast", or a number specifying a number of milliseconds.

The optional **callback** parameter is a function that will be executed after the hide() or show() method completes.

jQuery toggle()

With jQuery, you can toggle between the hide() and show() methods with the toggle() method. Visible elements are hidden and hidden elements become visible:

Example

```
$("button").click(function(){
  $("p.first()").toggle();
});
```

Syntax

```
$(selector).toggle(speed,callback);
```

Since toggle is really just calling the show or hide functions, it naturally offers the same parameters. The optional speed parameter can take the following values: "slow", "fast", or a number of milliseconds.

The optional callback parameter is the function to execute after toggle()

completes.

jQuery Fading

Instead of simply showing or hiding elements, jQuery also allows you to fade elements in and out of visibility. jQuery has the following fade methods:

- fadeIn()
- fadeOut()
- fadeToggle()
- fadeTo()

jQuery fadeIn() Method

The jQuery fadeIn() method is used to make a hidden element progressively more visible. When it finishes, the element is fully visible.

Syntax

```
$(selector).fadeIn(speed,callback);
```

The optional speed parameter specifies the duration of the effect. It accepts following values: "slow", "fast", or a number of milliseconds.

The optional callback parameter is a function to be executed after the fading completes.

jQuery fadeIn() Example

The following example demonstrates the fadeIn() method with different parameters:

```
$("button").click(function(){
```

```
  $("#div1").fadeIn();
  $("#div2").fadeIn("slow");
  $("#div3").fadeIn(5000);
});
```

jQuery fadeOut() Method

The jQuery fadeOut() method is used to make a visible element progressively less visible. When it finishes, the element is fully hidden.

Syntax

```
$(selector).fadeOut(speed,callback);
```

The optional speed parameter specifies the duration of the effect. It accepts following values: "slow", "fast", or a number of milliseconds.

The optional callback parameter is a function to be executed after the fading completes.

jQuery fadeOut() Example

The following example demonstrates the fadeOut() method with different parameters:

```
$("button").click(function(){
  $("#div1").fadeOut();
  $("#div2").fadeOut("slow");
  $("#div3").fadeOut(3000);
});
```

jQuery fadeToggle() Method

Similar to the jQuery toggle() method which toggles between the hide() and show() methods, The jQuery fadeToggle() method toggles between the fadeIn() and fadeOut() methods.

If the elements are hidden, fadeToggle() will fade them in.   If the elements are visible, fadeToggle() will fade them out.

Syntax

```
$(selector).fadeToggle(speed,callback);
```

The optional speed parameter specifies the duration of the effect. It accepts following values: "slow", "fast", or a number of milliseconds.

The optional callback parameter is a function to be executed after the fading completes.

jQuery fadeToggle() Example

The following example demonstrates the fadeToggle() method with different parameters:

```
$("button").click(function(){
  $("#div1").fadeToggle();
  $("#div2").fadeToggle("fast");
  $("#div3").fadeToggle(5000);
});
```

jQuery fadeTo() Method

The final option in the set of jQuery fade methods is the fadeTo() method. The fadeTo() method allows fading to a given opacity (and takes a value between 0 and 1). This is contrasted with the other fade in methods which always finish with showing the element at 100% opaque.

Syntax

```
$(selector).fadeTo(speed,opacity,callback);
```

The *required* speed parameter specifies the duration of the effect. It accepts following values: "slow", "fast", or a number of milliseconds.

The *required* opacity parameter in the fadeTo() method specifies fading to a given opacity (value between 0 and 1).

The *optional* callback parameter is a function to be executed after the fading completes.

jQuery fadeTo() Example

The following example demonstrates the fadeTo() method with different parameters:

```
$("button").click(function(){
  $("#div1").fadeTo("slow",0.15);
  $("#div2").fadeTo("slow",0.5);
  $("#div3").fadeTo("slow",0.8);
});
```

jQuery Sliding

The jQuery slide methods show or hide elements by sliding them up or down. jQuery has the following slide methods:

- slideDown()

- slideUp()

- slideToggle()

jQuery slideDown() Method

The jQuery slideDown() method is used to slide down an element into visibility.

Syntax

```
$(selector).slideDown(speed,callback);
```

The optional speed parameter specifies the duration of the effect. It can take the following values: "slow", "fast", or a number of milliseconds.

The optional callback parameter is a function to be executed after the sliding completes.

jQuery slideDown() Example

The following example demonstrates the slideDown() method:

```
$("#button").click(function(){
  $("#panel").slideDown();
});
```

jQuery slideUp() Method

The jQuery slideUp() method is used to slide up an element into invisibility.

Syntax

```
$(selector).slideUp(speed,callback);
```

The optional speed parameter specifies the duration of the effect. It can take the following values: "slow", "fast", or a number of milliseconds.

The optional callback parameter is a function to be executed after the sliding completes.

jQuery slideUp() Example

The following example demonstrates the slideUp() method:

```
$("#button").click(function(){
  $("#panel").slideUp();
});
```

jQuery slideToggle() Method

The jQuery slideToggle() method toggles between the slideDown() and slideUp() methods.

If the elements are visible, slideToggle() will slide them up.   If the elements are invisible, slideToggle() will slide them down into visibility.

Syntax

```
$(selector).slideToggle(speed,callback);
```

The optional speed parameter can take the following values: "slow", "fast", or a number of milliseconds.

The optional callback parameter is a function to be executed after the sliding completes.

jQuery slideToggle() Example

The following example demonstrates the slideToggle() method:

```
$("#button").click(function(){
  $("#panel").slideToggle();
});
```

jQuery Animate

The jQuery animate() method is used to create custom animations.   Nearly any CSS property can be animated however keep in mind that all property names must be camel-cased when used with the animate() method. For example you will need to write paddingRight instead of padding-righ, marginRight instead of margin-right, and so on.

> **Note**: By default all HTML elements have a static position and cannot be moved via animation.   To manipulate an elements position, remember to first set the CSS position property of the element to relative, fixed, or absolute.
>
> Color animation is not included in the core jQuery library. If you want to animate color, you need to download the Color Animations plugin from jQuery.com.

Syntax

```
$(selector).animate({params},speed,callback);
```

The required params parameter defines the CSS properties to be animated.

The optional speed parameter specifies the duration of the effect. It accepts following values: "slow", "fast", or a number of milliseconds.

The optional callback parameter is a function to be executed after the animation completes.

jQuery Animate Example

The following example demonstrates a simple use of the animate() method; it moves a <div> element to the right, until it has reached a left property of 300px:

```
$("button").click(function(){
  $("div").animate({left:'300px'});
});
```

Animating Multiple Properties

If you *really* want to get fancy, and I encourage you to use this in moderation, it is possible to animate multiple properties at the same time:

```
$("button").click(function(){
  $("div").animate({
    left:'250px',
    opacity:'0.7',
    height:'300px',
    width:'300px'
  }, "slow");
});
```

5657680R00085

Printed in Great Britain
by Amazon.co.uk, Ltd.,
Marston Gate.